# CREATIVITY
# *CYCLING*

*Help your team solve complex
problems with creative tools*

**Barbara A. Wilson & Tracy Stanley**

A CIP catalogue record for this book is available from the British Library and the National Library of Australia.

Paperback
ISBN-13: 978-0-6481892-4-4

Editor Desolie Page AE
Book design by adamhaystudio.com

We dedicate this book
to all leaders seeking to
boost the creativity of
their team as they solve
complex problems

# Contents

## LIST OF FIGURES

## LIST OF TABLES

# Is this book for you?

Creativity Cycling is written for leaders who want to help their team solve complex problems by applying creative thinking skills. These concepts could be new to you or you may have already been exposed to them. We believe this book will be of value if you want tools and processes you can use to lead your team through the creative problem solving process.

Many people have analytical tools they've acquired through formal studies or work experience that they apply when faced with a challenging situation. Indeed, organisations have extensive experience in applying rational and analytical skills such as data mining, correlation analysis, scenario analysis and forecasting, to name a few. These are all valuable and have their place.

From our experience, organisations sometimes lack knowledge or experience of using other tools and processes such as creative tools. In this book we describe our favourite creative exercises and how we've used them for solving complex problems and envisioning the future.

Sprinkled throughout the book are quotes from people we spoke to and who Tracy interviewed through her PhD research about creativity in the workplace. While their statements are real, their names are not.

# How to use this book

This book includes both practical and theoretical material. Parts 2, 3 and 4 will provide you with the theoretical background on the importance of creativity in the workplace and its added value for business. This context will allow you to effectively apply the practical processes and tools that are outlined in Part 5 in an easy-to use how to format.

*Creativity will become one of the top three skills workers will need by 2020*

World Economic Forum, 2016

*'How many of you would agree that the vast majority of the workforce possesses far more capability, creativity, talent, initiative and resourcefulness than their present job allows or requires them to use?' The affirmative answer is about 99 percent*

Question posed by Steven Covey (2010) in seminars

# Why is this book called Creativity Cycling?

We love metaphors. They help us imagine something from a different perspective, providing new insights. The bicycle and the act of cycling were the two metaphors we (eventually) selected for this book after we'd explored a number of ideas.

## What do a bike and a journey have to do with creative problem solving?

The bicycle is a vehicle to a destination of new ideas. The bike needs a solid framework. For us, this framework is built on openness, trust and mutual support. With a strong framework you feel safe to take the journey.

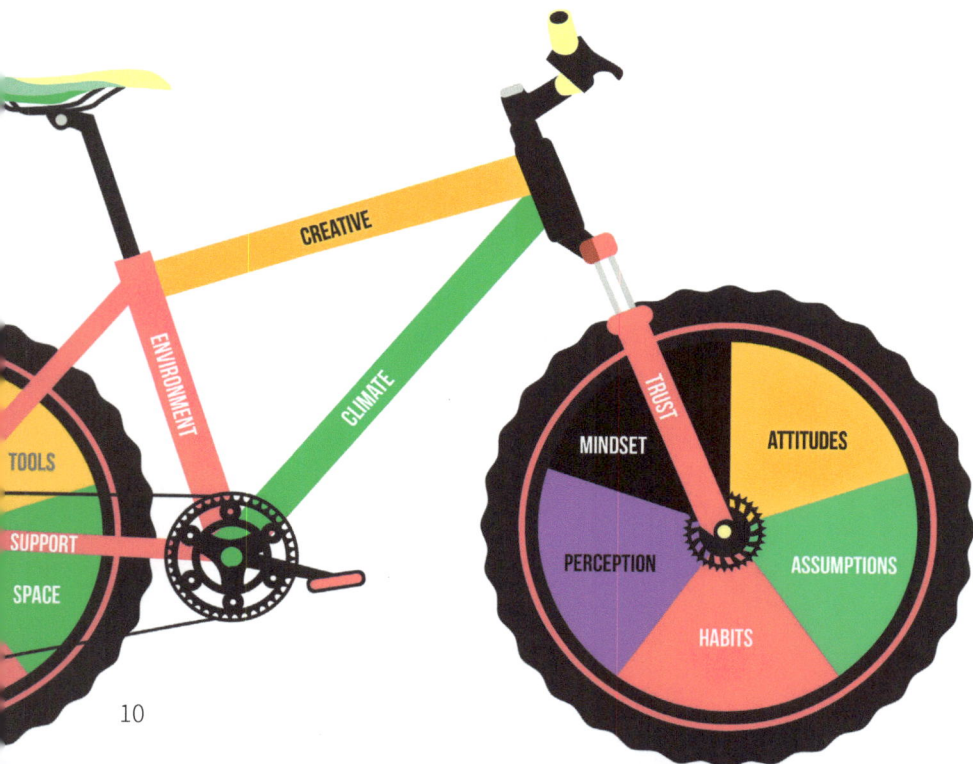

# The framework is supported by two wheels.

The front wheel encapsulates all the attitudes, habits and perceptions that we've developed throughout our life. What we've learnt in the past helps us but sometimes limits our thinking. The more conscious we are of this, the more open we will be to new insights.

The back wheel has the resources you need for the journey. These include the processes and tools that will help you to help your team think differently. Resources include time, space and other physical and people resources.

Once your bike is equipped you can set off on your journey. You may choose to cycle on your own, with someone else or in a peloton as a part of a race. So, there are many ways that you can travel to your destination with advantages and disadvantages associated with each method.

The creative problem solving process is itself a cycle, incorporating divergent (thinking wide) and convergent thinking (focusing and drawing conclusions). The process we'll refer to was developed by Alex Osborn. As this creative problem solving process cycle is at the heart of this book, we decided to call our book *Creativity Cycling*.

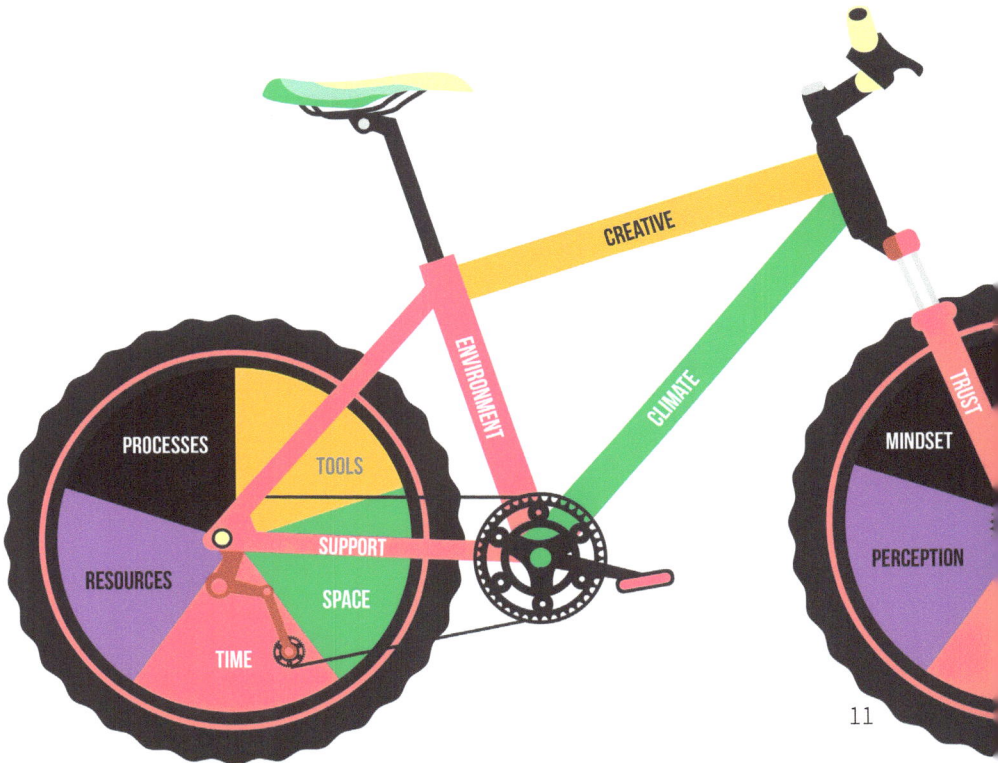

# How the book is organised

The book is organised into seven parts:

In Part 1 we discuss **what creativity is.** Like cycling, creativity can take many formats, from pleasurable meandering through the countryside to facing the toughest environment and competitors in the Tour de France. You could be trying to make incremental improvements in processes, or identifying new thinking or solutions to really difficult problems which we sometimes call wicked problems.

In Part 2 we discuss **why being creative** is important. We describe the business case for organisations investing in building creative thinking skills. In short, creative skills help people to identify opportunities as well as solve complex problems. We make the case for you as a leader, developing your own creative skills while facilitating the development of your team's skills.

In Part 3 we talk about the **power of assumptions, mindsets, habits and perceptions** and how these influence creative thinking.

Part 4 looks at how we **encourage learning** and creativity within the team environment. This part covers the team environment, both psychologically and physically, and the roles we can play. We also touch on culture, idea management processes and recruiting team members with an openness to creativity.

Part 5 provides the **tools and practices** which will support creativity in your team. We have a range of tools in our paniers to help you as you follow the divergent and convergent cycles within the creative problem solving process.

Part 6 looks at **your role as leader, coach and facilitator**.

Part 7 **wraps up** our key messages.

# **Part 1**
# Setting the scene

We wanted this book to be first and foremost useful: a valuable resource for leaders wishing to inject creativity into their team's thinking when faced with complex problems. Writing a jargon-free book was also important to us. There are enough books around using the latest management jargon. Finally, we wanted this book to be fun, beautiful and a demonstration of applied creative thinking.

*For every complex problem, there is an answer that is clear, simple, and wrong.*

H.L. Mencken

# 1.1 What is creativity?

**What did you do creatively this week?**

> *Did you use a new recipe when you cooked a meal, or invented a new recipe?*
>
> *Did you take a different route to work, or cycled rather than driving?*
>
> *Did you, as a leader, take decisions which were different to previous ones?*

All of these are examples of displaying creativity.
So, what is this thing called creativity?
It may be helpful firstly to define being creative.

One definition from the Collins English dictionary offers *having the ability to create, characterised by originality of thought; having or showing imagination, characterized by sophisticated bending of the rules or conventions.*

In this section we will encourage you to reflect upon different ways in which people display creativity, much as in the examples above. We'll look at adaptive creativity (which could be said to be about doing the same thing differently) compared to innovative creativity (which is about doing different things).

Before we go any further it's also important to talk about being creative versus being logical. Throughout this book we encourage you to think and act differently, try new ways of working, listen to your intuition and play with new ideas. It's often a play between the rational and the intuitive.

As a final word in this section, we emphasise the playfulness that enables creativity to happen. As we will see later in the book, play is essential in order to develop a looseness and a flexible approach that allows creativity to happen.

# 1.2 Different types of creativity (adaptive v innovative)

A firm belief we hold is that everyone has the capacity to be creative. Everyone expresses creativity in their own way. It's important to look for ways in which you can or do display **your** own creativity.

Michael Kirton developed an adaption/innovation theory to explain these differences in style. The theory is based upon two assumptions. The first is that creativity, decision making and problem solving are outcomes of the same brain function. The second assumption is that everyone is able to solve problems, take decisions and be creative. What differs is their style.

To use a cooking metaphor, some people are creative by taking a recipe, and changing or adapting it to suit their situation. They are called adaptors and work within existing structures, whereas other people are innovative and would be more inclined to design a whole menu from scratch, something that's a step outside of the usual structure. A contrast we could see as being either in-the-box or out-of-the-box thinking. Both are creative. There will be times when an adaptor approach is needed, or at other times, the innovator approach.

**OUT-OF-THE-BOX THINKING**

This type of thinking is a metaphor for creative thinking where it's encouraged to go beyond the boundaries. Its origin is believed to come from the well-known 9 dot puzzle shown below where you are asked: connect all nine dots using four straight lines or fewer, without lifting the pen and without tracing the same line more than once.

The answer is to go beyond the boundaries of the dots, as we show below. Staying within the boundaries of the nine dots would be a self-imposed rule, one that was never stated in the instructions.

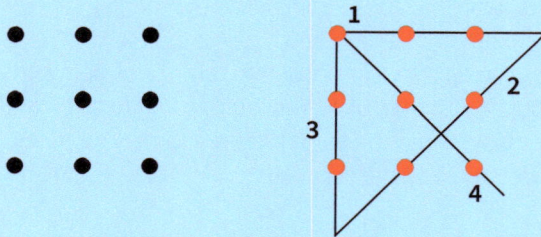

**Figure 1** Exercise illustrating 'Thinking outside the Box'

Kirton developed an instrument, KAI, to measure and define where someone falls on the spectrum of adaptor to innovator. It has proven useful in pulling together teams for work on creative projects. As with all differences in style, conflict can arise between people at either end of the spectrum. Adaptors may see innovators as too risky, argumentative, not focused, whereas adaptors may be seen as too methodical, and rule bound. However, as we see later in building teams to become creative teams, both styles are needed for diversity of thought and balance.

The idea of encouraging out-of-the-box ideas and working at the innovator end of the spectrum led to a surge of blue-sky thinking initiatives across organisations. Blue-sky thinking is a metaphor for opening up to totally new ideas. While it's not clear where the term originated, it was fashionable in the early 2000s and did lead to some interesting collaborations between global organisations, universities, and research centres to open up new approaches. On an everyday level, the adaptor type of approach may be more useful, that is working with what we already have and adapting the situation to develop our ideas for improvement. Continuous improvement, an idea that developed out of the Japanese Kaizen Concept, comes into this category.

> *The Kaizen Concept is a philosophy of continuous improvement of working practices that underlies total quality management and just-in-time business techniques.*
> Collins Dictionary

However, as we can see when we propose a creative problem solving process in Part 5, the more open innovator approach is extremely useful in tackling problems that are complex and have not been resolved easily in the past.

An alternative way of looking at these differences in being creative is to consider the reasons why creativity may be encouraged in organisations. This assumes an environment where creativity is encouraged, and this is not always the case – as we have discovered in our research and from our experience.

## 1.3 When and where to be creative

Creativity can happen anywhere and at any time.

However, as we see later in this book, preparing the ground to enable creativity is a valuable role for you as a leader. In doing this you might reflect upon the diverse ways and the places, both physical and in time, which can enable creativity.

As we saw in Part 1.1, there are several types of creativity or different ways of being creative. Many people have creative interests which they may leave behind when they enter the work environment. Others find ways, however small, to display creativity in their everyday life at work as well as at home. You only need to observe the differences people make to their workspaces.

Rare are the jobs which specifically require creativity as a skill. However, a creative-thinking or 'acting differently' mindset can be valuable in different scenarios in the workplace.

Some of these moments are listed below, (this list is not exhaustive):

- **When complex problems arise and require a different approach.**

- **When innovative ideas are needed because the old ones are no longer producing good results.**

- **When the market demands new thinking, for example when tastes change or technology changes. At this point an organisation will need to be innovative and new ideas should be encouraged from all parts of the organisation.**

- **When teams and organisations need inspiration for their future direction. We'll discuss visioning in Part 5.5, which may be helpful to explore in this type of situation.**

So, where can you be creative? Again, our answer would be - anywhere. However, we discuss space and creativity in Part 4.3 with some suggestions of how some spaces may be more conducive to creativity.

**Often the best places to be creative are not everyday work spaces.**
Changing your environment by going off site or moving into another more relaxed space, taking a walk, and playing sport are examples people have given as places where their ideas come from. As Sarah, one of our interviewees said:

> *Sports facilities allow people more freedom to take time out, meet, network, share ideas etc. People re-enter their working spaces often with new ideas.*

As a leader you can change the physical space where your team works and provide dedicated time to explore new ideas. Make sure you capture these ideas, which could initially be messy, so that they can be revisited in the future. There are many idea capture systems available, from hand scribbled or more formal notes, cameras, video recorders, proprietary knowledge capture systems (such as Bright Idea, IdeaDrop or Viima), to scribbling on a whiteboard.

Having looked at the different types of creativity and when it can happen we're now going to examine how our minds work and how we can develop a more open approach which will help us to become more creative.

# Part 2
# Why creativity?

By doing things differently we begin to open new pathways in our brain.

## 2.1 Reasons to develop your creativity

By working more creatively on a day-to-day basis, you will start to live your life differently, see things from different perspectives with results that will impact upon not only you individually but your work environment and team members. This can result in you and your team becoming more productive and effective at work as you challenge the old order in which things are done and search out new and better ways of doing them.

By choosing to work in a more creative way you'll find that you become more energised and interested in possible new and different outcomes. It has been shown that a more creative environment that engages people is motivating (Stanley, 2016). If you bring this sense of creativity into your work life as a leader or member of a team, you will start to see the world from different perspectives, which will open you up to all sorts of different opportunities.

By being creative in problem solving you'll find that complex problems start to be solved in a more effective way.

> *Complex problems require a different approach to solution finding.*

We often start to solve problems by making assumptions about the nature of the problem and we're very quick to reach a solution. This can and does frequently lead to a cycle of solving the wrong problem, and our original problem resurfaces. Creative problem solving enables and encourages you to see the big picture and not to go down the same road each time you encounter a problem.

By becoming more creative you will find that possibilities open up for you, your team and your organisation. There's a strong business case for creativity, especially when organisations need to be constantly changing and innovating in response to competitive and rapidly changing marketplaces. Creativity enables innovation and change to happen. If this is managed in an engaging climate, the innovation and change can be energising for the whole organisation.

*If you always do what you've always done, you'll always get what you've always got.*

Susan Jeffers, *Feel the Fear and Do it Anyway*

*One's mind, once stretched by a new idea, never regains its original dimension.*

Oliver Wendell Holmes Sr.

## 2.2 Motivational/Developmental for the individual

For many people overcoming a challenge is a bit like solving a puzzle. It stimulates curiosity combined with a desire to achieve something – to get the problem solved.

**Our minds like to play with possibilities.** It engages us. It's what Tracy's research (and that from many other studies) has revealed as typically present within an engaging job. A participant in Tracy's research echoed this sentiment in his comment:

> *The bigger challenges in our projects – these are the projects when I need to do my best thinking. John*

As we noted in the previous section, choosing to work creatively is energising and motivating. When using creative tools in my coaching and workshops, I have frequently seen that participants tend to engage and become more animated. I have numerous examples that energy seems to flow more freely when using image-based tools, for example.

When we're engaged and working creatively we can often be working in a state of 'flow'. Mihaly Csikzentmihalyi identified this state in his work on Flow. He described the concept of Flow as being a 'state of heightened focus and immersion in activities such as art, play and work'. We become totally absorbed by what we do to the extent that we have no capacity to pay attention to anything else.

When we work creatively we often lose sense of time and really begin to enjoy what we're doing. This can be true of artists, writers, and indeed any person who is exploring something they would describe as their passion. It can be true of engineers, academics, researchers, and even leaders! However, for the most part this sense of flow seems to be missing in the workplace. If you as a leader can create those conditions, you may be amazed at the results.

## 2.3 What holds back creative thinking?

From our experience and research, we know that a willingness or cautiousness to engage in creative thinking can come from a person's education, cultural background, and socialisation. As a result, some people need encouragement to engage in creative thinking. You may need to give your team members both permission and the opportunity to engage in thinking differently. These are all BIG influencers.

Numerous writers and academics have noted that the education system, especially in the west, can reduce a child's ability to be creative. Ken Robinson is one such writer who, in a 2006 TED talk on creativity and schools, stated:

> *Picasso once said that all children are born artists. The problem is to remain an artist as we grow up. I believe this passionately, that we don't grow into creativity, we grow out of it. Or rather, we get educated out if it.*

So why is this?
It's hard to measure creativity, it's not the same as measuring IQ; this may be the reason that there's less emphasis in the system on developing it. We put a strong emphasis in our schools on thinking logically and rationally. As we don't live in a rational and logical world, this must be causing a lot of cognitive dissonance with many people.

**Creative thinking and its outputs are neither right nor wrong.**
If we're being creative and produce what we see as a creative output, the world around us may not agree: that's a barrier to being creative.

Observe how many of our now famous painters were treated in their lifetime. Cezanne sold very few of his paintings and even after his death, his native town of Aix en Provence in France was not interested in his legacy. When you go there, few of his paintings are displayed in the museums. The belief that Cezanne was misunderstood as a painter in his lifetime leads to another theory around creativity.

While anyone can be creative, whether or not it leads to recognition and innovation, depends upon external variables such as acceptance by the domain and marketplace. Think about the many examples in the commercial world of creative efforts turning into innovations that were not acceptable to the market. Sinclair's electric car produced in the UK in the mid-1980s was just one such example.

*My contention is that creativity now is as important in education as literacy, and we should treat it with the same status.*

*Ken Robinson*

The design was not acceptable to the marketplace and the market was not ready for electric cars. However, that should not stop teams working creatively.

In order to work creatively, it's important that the team are working collaboratively as a baseline from which to move to more radical ways of working.

## 2.4 Takeaways: Why creativity?

- The ability to think differently is an essential skill for employees.

- Complex problems require a different approach to problem solving.

- Using a creative problem solving process can help problems be solved more effectively.

- There is a strong business case for creativity in organisations.

- Our minds like to play with possibilities, and big problems can stretch our thinking and engage us.

- People sometimes need encouragement to engage in creative thinking.

**REFLECTION POINTS**

**Think about those things that may have shaped peoples' behaviours, such as education or cultural background and how it might influence differences in thinking.**

**Reflect on the different ways you can encourage your team to think differently.**

# Part 3
# Enabling creativity in your team

Who is a creative person that you admire?
How do/did they act that is different to others?
Picasso, or the prolific musician Brian Eno, or
modern-day innovators like Elon Musk may come
to mind.

When we try to understand the characteristics of 'creative' people, we soon find a range of individual attributes that define them as different. An obvious one which can relate to all three people we just mentioned is a passion for what they do or did.

Here we will be looking at some of these individual characteristics with the aim of helping you, as a leader, to encourage your team to be creative, as well as reviewing your own individual contribution.

One framework I particularly like (and this is Barbara speaking) is a model of individual conditions for creativity developed by Jane Henry, one of the authors of the Open University Business School MBA module *Creativity, Innovation and Change*. It claims that the important conditions for creativity can be summarised by 4 Ps:

## Positivity

*When we're positive we're open to new experiences and see opportunities for new learning. We're less likely to be focused on failure.*

## Playfulness

*A mind that is flexible, open to ambiguity, and able to see the world through different perspectives makes for playfulness.*

## Passion

*The motivation and commitment needed to work creatively requires passion. Observe how artists work when they are in the flow: their passion keeps them going.*

## Persistence

*Creativity can take time, and needs persistence. This shows through in examples such as the development of the Post-it, which was based upon an invention made in 1968, developed in 1974, and finally marketed in 1980.*

## The Psychology of Creativity

Why do some people appear more open to ideas than others? Why are some people more negative about change? I am sure that you, as a leader, will have at some time considered these questions.

It may be that differences can be explained by individual personality and/or life experiences. However, there may be psychological explanations for differences in behaviour that can be addressed. In this section I am going to introduce you to some of these. We'll look at the explanations so that you can learn more about why differences in the way people process information occur, and what you can do to challenge them. The model, based upon the work of Chris Argyris, helps to explain how our perceptions, beliefs and attitudes influence each other in a reinforcing way.

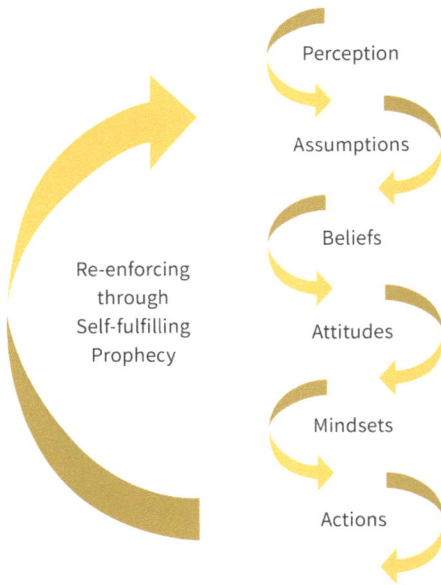

Perception

Assumptions

Beliefs

Re-enforcing
through
Self-fulfilling
Prophecy

Attitudes

Mindsets

Actions

**Figure 2** Constructing and Deconstructing Mindsets (Wilson, 2018)

When we observe something, we select from the observation, interpret to add meaning and then make assumptions that lead to beliefs and that may turn into actions. I believe we have all seen this process at work. Lots of examples could be shared here, many of them quite controversial and which have led to issues like discrimination in the workplace.

Working through Figure 2, we will look at each of the concepts in turn and note how they influence each other.

## 3.1 Perception

Perception is about how we see our world, and it's subjective. My perception will differ from yours, even if we may have some similarities due to our upbringing or background.

We all have a need to make sense of our surroundings and interpret what is happening, so we look for familiar signs and patterns. When faced with the unfamiliar we interpret what we perceive in terms of our prior experiences and fill in any gaps accordingly.

**Here's an example:**
As a leader you are aware that a member of your team – let's call them Joss – is leaving work earlier than normal on a regular basis. Your experience is that people who leave early are no longer really motivated by their job, so you start to watch Joss more closely. You notice that he no longer joins the rest of the team for lunch, and then one day he arrives more smartly dressed than normal for work. By this time, you have interpreted a whole lot of signs and patterns in accordance with your past experiences, making the assumption that Joss is disengaged and is probably going for interviews elsewhere. If you do not challenge your assumptions at this point and have a friendly chat with him, you may start to act on the picture you have built up in your mind and the next time an interesting task arises you might exclude him. When you do get around to talking to him, he has been put out by your less than friendly attitude towards him. It's almost too late when you discover that he has problems at home as a parent and the smarter dress was to make an impression on his child's teacher that evening.

Other people may have interpreted Joss's action differently. However, the important point here is that each of us will see our world differently, according to previous experiences.

## 3.2 Assumptions

In the example in 3.1, we see how important it is to challenge our assumptions. One way we encourage you to do this when working creatively is to seek others' perceptions of a situation. This is one good reason for staying open and working with diverse teams.

We all make assumptions on a daily basis and although some may turn out to be accurate, others might not.

*No two people see the external world in exactly the same way. To every separate person a thing is what he thinks it is -- in other words, not a thing, but a think.*

Penelope Fitzgerald

Assumptions do serve a genuine purpose. They short circuit the thinking and decision-making process, something that can be helpful in our daily lives. As a leader though, you may wish to ask yourself if your assumptions are well founded. Challenging your own assumptions is a great start to enabling creativity. It opens up new thinking.

So, what exactly are assumptions? They are part of our attitude-building mental process. The Oxford dictionary defines an assumption as '... *a thing that is accepted as true or as certain to happen, without proof.' For example,*

'We're working on the assumption that the time of death was after midnight.'

We need to be very careful about the assumptions we make. In the example above an assumption can be useful as a working position to start with, with the proviso that evidence will then be found to justify it. As long as the evidence is as objectively handled as possible and does provides a challenge to the original assumption, then a healthy conclusion can be reached.

So, to challenge your own assumptions you will need to move back through the sequence in Figure 2 and review the way in which you interpreted your perceptions of the situation. This is very much like opening up cold cases and re-examining all the original evidence collected. Were the correct interpretations made? Perhaps new evidence contradicts previous assumptions. Often new ways of thinking enable a new interpretation to be made.

One way to challenge our assumptions is the use of **Fresh-eye**. Fresh-Eye is an approach to creativity that encourages new perspectives. It's a way of challenging the accepted view of the situation, and to challenge the assumptions inherent in the situation. The approach is to change the perspective through which something is viewed and can be done by varying the techniques used and/or the people involved. Sometimes all it needs is the fresh eye of someone who knows nothing about the situation and has not bought into the perspectives around the issue. Think of the Hans Christian Anderson fairy tale *The Emperor's New Clothes, where it takes a child to challenge the perception everyone has bought into that the emperor is wearing a magnificent set of clothes when in fact he is naked.*

*When challenging assumptions at the problem-exploration stage of the Creative Problem Solving process encourage a Fresh-Eye approach by including people who have little or no knowledge of the problem or issue.*

By challenging our assumptions, we can begin to think differently and develop new ideas. Challenging other people's assumptions is more difficult. As a leader you may believe that someone is acting on what you consider to be an inaccurate assumption. If so, it's not wise to challenge in a confrontational way but rather challenge the assumption through a 'coaching' approach. Query the evidence to support the assumption you are seeing, and explore an alternative way of viewing the situation.

## 3.3 Beliefs and Attitudes

Our assumptions about something become beliefs over time. For example, you may believe that older people are more stuck in their ways than younger people. This may be based upon your prior perceptions and the assumptions you have developed. Now reflect upon how that belief translates in your mind into an attitude you have about older people and even how your behaviour is shaped by this attitude.

Attitudes are stronger than beliefs and incorporate feelings which can strengthen over time. They often serve a useful purpose by allowing us to make decisions without having to stop and reflect, acting like a fight or flight response. If we are in a jungle and we hear the roar of a lion, we don't stop to wonder if what we're hearing poses a threat - we just react. However, we don't spend our lives, or at least most of us don't, in a jungle. What may be appropriate as a fight or flight response in the jungle is not appropriate in the workplace.

### *Attitudes develop into mindsets, or habitual ways of thinking*

Mindsets are created when we develop attitudes based on our assumptions as you can see in Figure 2. They develop based on the relatively fixed ways in which we see our worlds.

Once established, our attitudes can lead to action, or behaviour towards an object. If that object is a person, our behaviour towards them can result in a self-fulfilling prophecy. For example, the recipient of our 'unfriendly' attitude responds in a negative fashion which reinforces our beliefs.

## 3.4 Mindsets

Eventually our beliefs grow into mindsets, which are overarching sets of habits and attitudes that can be built around self, as well as beliefs about our external world.

*Being creative requires a positive mindset, being open to new possibilities, being playful and ready to explore options.*

Let's briefly explore mindsets that are open and those that are limiting and which can influence creativity in teams.

The first of these is the **Growth versus Fixed mindset**.

Carol Dweck sets out an overview of this mindset in her book *The New Psychology of Success*. The **Fixed mindset** is a belief that life's experiences can be measured in success or failure. The **Growth mindset** assumes that we can all grow and develop, and any failure is an opportunity to do this.

> *In creative thinking, a growth mindset is needed in order to be open to new possibilities and to be open to risk and 'failing', because that's how we move on and develop.*

A fixed mindset is less likely to take risks if success is not assured.

The second mindset that is crucial in creative thinking is a **Positive versus a Negative** mindset.

Positivity – symbolised by a 'yes and' rather than a 'yes but' attitude – changes our demeanour. We become more agreeable, more confident and we engage better with others.

This is not advocating an utopian existence where we all go around smiling and agreeing with one another – some level of conflict is unavoidable when we work in diverse teams. However, if we are positive we handle conflict better. We're able to listen and reflect upon what we're hearing rather than jumping to conclusions. It's the difference between being realistic with an open mindset to being routinely negative. Negativity can draw us into a downwards spiral and become a self-fulfilling prophecy where we end up with what we expected.

We're all aware of the expression, 'a glass half-full or half-empty'. It's a useful metaphor for reflecting on whether your mindset is positive or negative. The way you perceive life will influence your actions. A life-half-full person will be more inclined to be open and embrace new possibilities. A life-half-empty person will be more inclined to see the world in a more pessimistic manner. Becoming or developing your creativity needs a half-full mindset, that is positive, rather than negative.

# 3.5 Habits

Do you always take the same route to work every day? What would happen if you changed your mode of travel or your route?

It's likely that initially it will be a little strange as a habit has been fixed for your journey. However, it will be interesting to observe the difference it makes.

Habits, as neuroscientists tell us, come about because we form neural pathways in our brain. This creates a short circuit to our behaviours so that we can do something without thinking too consciously about it. On a daily basis this is very efficient. I don't have to think too hard in a morning about what actions I'll take and in which order, as I've developed a routine for my first hour or so out of bed. This frees my brain to work on other things that may be more important.

However, habits can be a negative force on creativity when they prevent us from trying something different or thinking differently.

Habitual thinking can be negative and can lead to reactions at work such as 'this won't work, we have tried it before', or 'yes but', when anyone suggests something new. As a leader, you need to be aware of any such habits that you have and their impact, as well as observing them in your team. If these negative habits set in, it can be difficult to break them, but not impossible.

> *Breaking habits that are no longer serving us well requires a persistent and sustained approach.*

We need to consider what purpose the habit serves. Maybe it's fear of the unknown and we're using it as a defence. Once the habit is acknowledged and brought into the conscious, we need to replace it with a different and more positive habit. A good example is to challenge the 'yes but' with a 'yes and'. This habit needs to be practised because it's only by taking action and reinforcing new habits through repetition that they will gradually replace the old unwanted ones.

# 3.6 Thinking differently

### The role of the unconscious in the creative process

We can think of the mind as having two states, the conscious and the unconscious. Research by Guy Claxton suggests that the conscious mind lags behind the unconscious, and it's the unconscious mind that learns, thinks, takes decisions and solves problems.

Guy Claxton differentiated two kinds of thinking which he summed up in his book Hare Brain, Tortoise Mind. He identifies hare brain thinking as being about reasoning, 'cleverness' in coming up with a quick answer. While the tortoise mind takes longer to get to an 'answer', it allows the unconscious mind to work, allows hunches to appear, and more and better ideas to emerge. Claxton suggests that when a decision has to be made we ask what the deadline is. Then we make the decision just before the deadline. This allows the unconscious tortoise mind to work. If the decision is taken straight away as it often is in business, it may be an acceptable decision but not necessarily the best.

As a leader you may be aware of making decisions based upon your intuition. Research backs up the case for leaders with experience making better judgements when using their intuition. This is an important differentiator to consider. The inexperienced intuitive is not necessarily going to make good decisions because intuition relies on the unconscious learning and experience that has been accumulated over time. The decisions that are taken intuitively are often justified later by the conscious mind and rational explanation. However, this intuition really comes into its own when handling complexity, which is what is needed for creative problem solving.

> *The process of using intuition*
> *often requires incubation.*

Haven't we all experienced times when the answer is on the tip of your tongue but you can't access it. A period of incubation often has the effect of bringing it from the unconscious to the conscious mind.

Incubation can also be an important factor in creativity when we get stuck. Taking a break, doing something different, and then coming back to the issue is very helpful in the process of creative problem solving. In the meantime, your unconscious brain will continue to analyse the information, so allow it the time to do this.

*So if you have two ideas ... then it really is down to preference ... Sometimes we will have a difference in preference which will result in many discussions. And I encourage this as it actually suits my thought processes and I try and put it down and come back the next day. I always find that my sub-conscious tends to do a whole lot of work in the background. It doesn't let my conscious know until the next day. Brian*

**Left Brain/Right Brain**

This difference is an important one to consider in the context of creativity. It has become fairly commonplace to equate creative thinking with right brain activity and logical, rational thinking with the left brain. However, research on the brain suggests that this is perhaps too simplistic, and that while there is some evidence that different brain hemispheres control different aspects of the body, such as language, there is no evidence for the link with creativity and logical thinking.

The conclusion we reach here is that while left brain/right brain is a useful metaphor for the two different ways of thinking, it's not to be taken literally.

## 3.7 Takeaways: Enabling creativity in your team

- Be mindful of the 4 Ps: Positivity, Playfulness, Passion and Persistence.

- Mindsets are created when we develop beliefs based on our assumptions.

- In creative thinking a growth mindset is important.

- Your conscious mind may be lagging behind your unconscious mind. You may need to give your team (and your own mind) time to incubate their ideas.

**REFLECTION POINTS**

**How do you identify and challenge your own assumptions?**

**What steps can you take to create positive and playful attitudes?**

It's now time to turn our attention to the characteristics in your team's work environment that influence creativity, and the roles we can play as we apply a creative process.

# Part 4
# Building a creative team environment

This part considers how to create the best environment to encourage creativity …

It's a bit like setting up a greenhouse so that seedling plants get the sunshine and water that they need, as well as protection from harsh environmental conditions, as illustrated in Figure 3. This part also considers the impact of physical space, time, and diverse team roles.

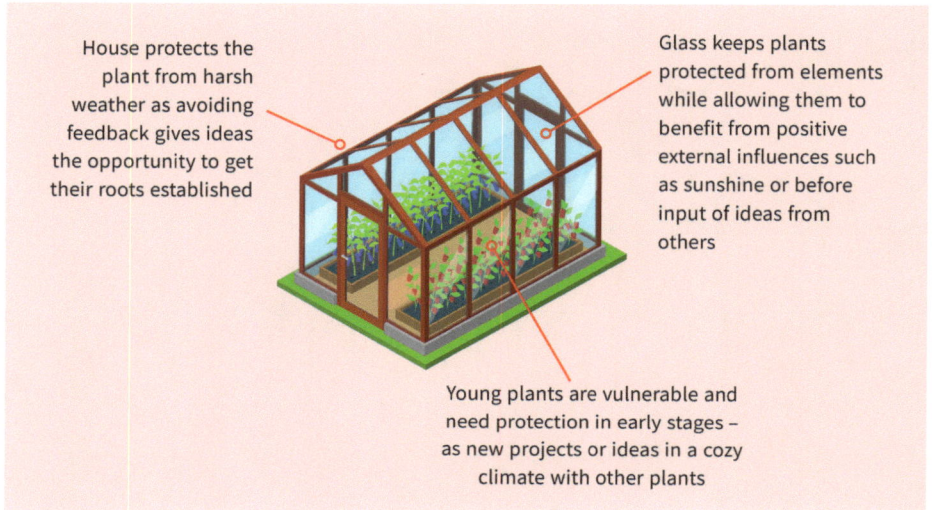

House protects the plant from harsh weather as avoiding feedback gives ideas the opportunity to get their roots established

Glass keeps plants protected from elements while allowing them to benefit from positive external influences such as sunshine or before input of ideas from others

Young plants are vulnerable and need protection in early stages – as new projects or ideas in a cozy climate with other plants

**Figure 3** Metaphor for Greenhouse of ideas

## 4.1 Creating a creative work environment

### *There's something in the air tonight.*

Heard this expression before? It alludes to something encouraging people to behave in a certain way. It's not easy to see, although people's actions give you a clue. And you certainly can feel it. Well the 'it' is the environment – and there are many things that influence the environment.

How you feel in any environment will influence how you behave. As a leader you want to create an environment where people feel safe to explore different ideas and approaches to solving a problem.

### *In a creative work environment, your team members will be curious, ask lots of questions and seek out new information.*

They will experiment, with failure being recognised as a learning point from which they capture knowledge and continue with the problem solving process. Failure should not be seen as fatal. With a need to solve increasingly difficult problems, your team will benefit from an environment where collaboration and continuous learning is the normal way of working.

## What is a work environment?

Let's get our definitions on the table. A work environment has two broad types of characteristics, including the social-organisational and the physical environment characteristics, according to Dul and Ceynan. The first group covers stuff like the design of jobs, working style of the leader and the psychological aspects, i.e. how safe people are feeling in terms of trust and openness. The second group looks at the office setup and surrounding buildings. We talk a bit more about the design of physical space shortly in Section 4.3

Work environments influence if and how your team will generate new and useful ideas – so it's worth looking at your team's working space and thinking about how team members would describe the environment in the team. There's been research in this space from Amabile, Conti, Coon, Lazenby and Herron and Scott & Bruce.

Behaviours that build a great work environment for creativity include helping each other, seeking help when you need it and rethinking or reframing a problem so that it can be viewed differently. These behaviours often happen together and are typical of a team working in a collaborative manner. While new ideas can be discovered accidentally, according to Unsworth and Clegg, most will come out of a process that is intentional and deliberately undertaken. So, think about your processes as well as your work environment if you want it to boost creative thinking.

## Challenges stimulate creative thinking

Many things influence the work environment. The nature of work undertaken and the types of challenges faced will reveal areas where creative thinking skills are particularly useful. Facing a problem could be a catalyst for the application of problem solving skills, as revealed in the following.

> *When they are challenging I think – that brings out innovation: how to research – how to manage the problems. Vasken*

Indeed, solving problems is one of the characteristics that often makes a job valuable.

> *I actually do enjoy it. I like getting to the bottom of things. Lisa*

Solutions to problems often emerge through discussions with colleagues about the source of the problem and possible ways forward. An individual retaining ownership of the solution to the problem is also important for empowerment, although others may offer suggestions.

Challenging problems help your team develop a range of skills, and if they are successful in solving a challenging problem, they receive a wonderful sense of accomplishment.

**You're a role model**

As a leader and coach your behaviour is key. Your team will watch you closely and are likely to model your behaviours. If, for example, you track trends, are curious, and spend time exploring different ideas, then your team are likely to copy you. Offering encouragement and resources signals support for new ways of doing things. As a role model, your approach should be to empower rather than to instruct. Offer support first and advice second.

**Autonomy is important for ownership**

Giving your team members freedom and autonomy in how they undertake their work is very important for creativity. As a leader, your relationship with your team members and their positive attitudes towards new ways of working is a key influencer on their willingness and openness to explore new ideas. Resist the urge to meddle or micro-manage their activities and give praise and feedback to encourage further exploration of an idea.

And listening, of course, is important too.

Along with autonomy it's imperative for you as a leader to remove the things that may limit your team's capacity to undertake their work. These could be organisational impediments:

> *Look it's probably one of the things that the business prides itself on – the very little structural impediments to doing something. It's funny because I used to go around the world doing a lot of planning and training and stuff like that – you'd hear people working on businesses for the most obscure things. People can do what they want. That is why the company has 280 patents for technology. ... Alpha is very different and one of the key differences to many of its competitors ... and the only way you can do this is to allow people a lot of freedom. Ideas like I said at the start, it is easier to ask for forgiveness than permission. Chris*

*Your goal should be to empower them to make decisions.*

It's interesting to note the statement that it's easier to ask for forgiveness than for permission, and the clear sense of allowing people time to 'play' with ideas. What's the culture like in your organisation regarding investing in not-yet-approved ideas? Is there time to play with these ideas?

### Time and resources for creativity

Having enough time to explore a problem and to consider alternatives supports the discovery of new approaches. Ideas need a period of incubation in order to gestate. In his book *Where good ideas come from: The Natural history of innovation, Steven Johnson calls this 'the slow hunch' theory: a great idea slowly fades into view over a long period of time. He provides the example of Charles Darwin and his theory of natural selection.*

Time is a curious thing. If you have no time to think and to experiment, you will do an activity exactly as you always have. You have no choice. However, if you have too much time you may lack focus:

> **One aspect is time. If I'm given enough time, normally I perform a little better. But too much time is also not very good (laughs); just the right amount of time. Jorge**

My PhD research (Tracy speaking here) confirmed the findings of others that there is a 'sweet spot' with regard to the right amount of time to support creative behaviours. Here's how I illustrate the sweet spot.

**Time Pressure and Creative Bevaviours**

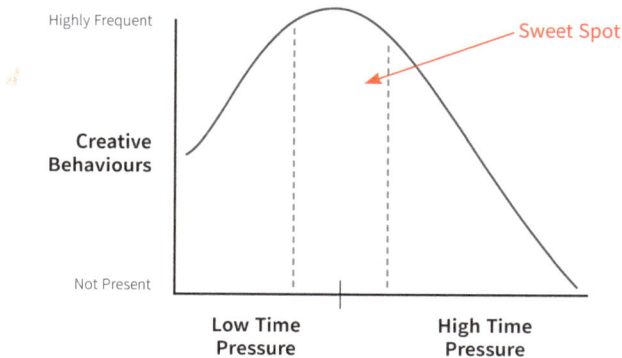

**Figure 4** Illustration of 'Sweet Spot' for time pressure (Stanley, 2016)

It's somewhat helpful to highlight how no time pressure could lead to boredom and nothing being done, with too little time also leading to nothing being done as there's no time for reflection and incubation. Similarly, there's a need to strike the right balance in the provision of resources to support creativity. Csikszentmihalyi suggests that resources can make individuals too comfortable, which can have a deadening effect on creativity. Resources could include budget, people and physical assets. As a leader and motivator, you have a balancing act to play here.

I can't help but think about hackathons and the value they provide in stimulating creative thinking. They include the essential component of time pressure to deliver. But it's not this characteristic alone which leads to success: it's a combination of teams with motivated, curious and energetic people willing to follow a process of discovery, evaluation, probable failure and learning – while being chased by a clock to deliver.

### Differing viewpoints on time pressure

Hopefully you'll have people with different views in your team. I'll illustrate this point through a conversation Barbara and I had when writing this chapter about time pressure.

**Tracy** I think events such as hackathons are useful for forcing creative analysis through a focused, time-pressurised, fun and collaborative process.

**Barbara** I agree that the collaboration that comes through hackathons is valuable and particularly well suited to people who are highly extroverted. In any team there are likely to be people who process their ideas through quiet reflection. As with any process you should consider both the positive and negative aspects. I would suggest that the question of time needs to take into consideration the objectives of the creativity. Some creative ideas can take time and it may be useful for their 'owners' to work underground on them over time rather than have to come up with them in a tight time frame.

**Tracy** Good reminder about different styles Barbara. As an extrovert I love this type of event and sometimes forget that they don't suit everyone. My comment also came from recognising that I can procrastinate and overthink things. A bit of time pressure helps me to get my skates on.

**Barbara** Many of us are procrastinators Tracy. Procrastination serves a useful purpose in that it allows time for ideas to incubate and form and reform. The final result may be a lot richer had it not been for that procrastination.

### People want to feel safe

It probably won't surprise you to learn that positive social relationships create a work environment where creativity can flourish. This is because when people feel psychologically safe, they can be open as they trust others and are comfortable experimenting and playing with an idea, as well as admitting that they've failed. Here's an insight from a participant in Tracy's research.

> *I think when people are joking around with each other and feel free to, you know, if someone's made a mistake they'll just go: Oh you've done that wrong. I think that everyone's really happy when no one seems to be protecting their own job worrying about if their making a mistake or asking a stupid question.* **Morgan**

You can sometimes 'hear' a team with a positive social environment as people feel at ease with one another which can generate friendly conversations and laughter. Where there are positive social relationships there are higher levels of collaboration. We talk a great deal about collaboration in this book, because while many ideas can come when you're on your own, the idea generation process is often richer when done with others.

> *I suppose we bounce ideas off each other and say: Do you have this problem when doing this? Is there any way? ... Has anyone thought of? ... Have you got that problem and how did you cope with that?* **Marie**

To recap some of the learning here, you as a leader can create an environment that is characterised by openness, in which experimentation is encouraged, and failure is accepted as a normal part of the learning process.

### Diversity adds dynamism

Diversity of background brings diversity of perspectives and ideas. Diversity can relate to cultural background, education and work experience to name a few. How diverse the background of your team members is will influence the diversity of ideas – so bear this in mind when recruiting new team members. Similarly, think about the diversity of functions and roles that should be involved when you're examining a problem that impacts many parts of the organisation. If you're facilitating a problem-solving event, invite representatives from those areas and sprinkle them across the different teams. Yes, the process may take longer but it will obtain a better result in terms of quality of ideas and buy-in to a final outcome. When we work with the same people, we get used to how they think and as a group we may all end up thinking the same way. It's good to shake that up.

Diversity can also be important in terms of thinking and communicating styles. Here (and this is Barbara speaking again) I want to look at two frameworks which can be helpful in understanding diversity in teams when putting together creative teams or managing the effects of diversity. Let's look first at the MBTI framework.

Myers Briggs offers a way of differentiating peoples' styles based on their behaviour and habitual responses to the environment; this is measured by their instrument the MBTI. While there has been some criticism of the MBTI instrument, I recommend using the framework as a way to review the types of behaviour that people exhibit in teams and to look for a balance of behaviours.

As you can see from the table 1 below, the MBTI offers four dimensions on which behaviour can be 'assessed'.

| TABLE 1 OVERVIEW OF DIMENSIONS OF MYERS BRIGGS TYPE INDICATORS | | |
| --- | --- | --- |
| Dimension | Behaviour | Focus |
| Extraversion/introversion | How you relate to others | People and things v. ideas and impressions |
| Sensing/Intuition | How you gather information | Information from the senses, and in the present v. future, patterns and possibilities |
| Thinking/Feeling | The way you make decisions | Logic and objective analysis v. values and subjective evaluation |
| Judging/Perceiving | The way you live your life | Planned and organised v. spontaneous, keeping options open |

## So, what are the implications for creativity?

Similar in lots of ways to Belbin (which I will talk about shortly), stages of the process suit some styles better than others; a balance is needed in a creative team. For example, the Introvert is likely to come up with great ideas, however they may be reluctant to share these in a team setting, and may be slower at formulating their ideas. Therefore, you need to plan creativity exercises with space for the introvert to contribute.

In divergent stages, the Perceptive type behaviour is needed in order to open up to possibilities.

The Judging type, especially in the divergent phases, may close them down too soon as they'll be uncomfortable when confronted with many options.

The Intuitive type is suited to early divergent stages, when imaging techniques may be used, whereas the Sensing type is extremely useful at later convergent stages when detail becomes important.

Having a diverse range of styles in a team can be challenging. Clashes and conflicts can easily arise in creative problem solving between people with different styles. This will need careful handling in any facilitation. It will be important to establish sound ground rules for any creativity process. Both these topics are discussed later in Part 5, when we look at the Creative Problem Solving process.

For more information on the MBTI, take a look at http://www.myersbriggs.org/my-mbti-personality-type/mbti-basics/

## 4.2 The roles we play in supporting creativity

### How different roles support creativity
In addition to the MBTI framework we've just looked at, it may be useful to consider another aspect of diversity: the roles we play in a team.

Dr Meredith Belbin developed this framework of team roles in the seventies, while studying the makeup of successful teams. Contrary to expectation he found that successful teams were made up of a diversity of people who took different roles.

This challenged his prior belief that successful teams would be made up of members who all shared high intellect. Belbin identified nine different roles, as shown in Table 2, based on clusters of behaviours of team members. He found that typically, people had tendencies matching several team roles. At the same time, they often had least preferred roles where they would be most uncomfortable if they had to 'play' this role in a team. For a team to be successful Belbin would argue that all roles need to be covered, even if several roles are covered by the same person. The nine roles are divided by their orientation:

| TABLE 2  BELBIN'S NINE ROLES SUPPORTING CREATIVITY | | | |
|---|---|---|---|
| Action-oriented roles | Shaper | Implementer | Completer-finisher |
| People-oriented roles | Co-ordinator | Team worker | Resource investigator |
| Thinking-oriented roles | Plant | Monitor-evaluator | Specialist |

In terms of creativity, what is particularly interesting with Belbin's roles is that some are considered to be more creative roles than others and function better at different stages of the creative/innovation process. For example:

The **Plant** is needed at the start or in the divergent phases of the creative problem solving process, to come up with great ideas.

The **Resource Investigator** is also a divergent creative role, in that they work outside the team looking for resources and connections.

The convergent and later stages of creative problem solving and innovation call for roles such as the **Monitor-evaluator, Completer-finisher** and **Implementer**.

An unbalanced team, for example not having anyone displaying tendencies of key roles such as the Plant, or having too many Plants, can lead to difficulties. Conflict can arise at the beginning of the process when there is more than one Plant, or perhaps low energy when there are too many Implementers or Completer-Finishers. If the convergent roles dominate in the divergent phases or vice versa, the creative process could either fail to take off in any meaningful way or could fail to find closure.

For more information on team roles I encourage you to check out Belbin's website. http://www.belbin.com/about/belbin-team-roles/

*The space we inhabit influences our thinking.*

## 4.3 How space influences creativity

Have you ever stood up to make an important phone call? How did it feel when you did, and how did it compare to sitting at your desk to make the call? If you haven't tried it, give it a go and note the difference. Standing or sitting, walking, cycling, driving or playing sports of some sort are all examples of physical space being used differently. In each situation we will start to think differently. Have you for example ever had that 'aha' moment in the shower?

Sitting at a desk encourages logical, rational thinking. While this is important in some parts of the creative cycle, it's not conducive to new, more intuitive thinking. Being seated at a table rather than say, standing around a flip chart, seems to diminish energy and the group looks to one person to lead. When all the group are in a more energised space, everyone seems enabled to contribute. So, the physical environment is a very important element in enabling our creative juices to flow. Some organisations have identified and implemented this practice: Google have designed their workspace to inspire creativity, and David Kelley, founder of IDEO, believes that there is strong relationship between physical space and creativity. Taking their inspiration from Google, one of our interviewees had this to contribute:

> *Closed offices have been opened in the new facility and have allowed more interaction between people. Walls/windows have pens which can be used to draw/write on them, coffee is free and available, and people are taking opportunities to share ideas over coffee. Sarah*

**What does this mean for the workplace and especially for creativity?**
If we want to encourage people to think differently or, to use the well-known metaphor, *think outside the box*, it's advisable that they are physically in a different space. Traditionally, creative thinking workshops are held off site, which may not be realistic if restricted by small budgets. So how can you create an atmosphere where people can be in a different physical space? The essential element to consider is how to work without desks.

The next time you need to do something creative, for example brainstorm, try changing the physical space. A simple solution is to go for a walk with the team. Many workplaces are being adapted to encourage creativity. We all know about Google and how space is allowed for play and free thinking. Other workplaces, such as the one referred to in one of our interviews, are encouraging more moments for physical, informal interaction, such as around the coffee machine.

In addition to physical space we might also consider emotional space. If people are feeling stressed for example, their minds will not be open, or could even be in panic mode. Reflect upon the team's emotional state. An emotionally healthy team will be much more creative. Sometimes it's necessary to take the time to detach oneself from the actual day-to-day work to get some emotional freedom to work creatively.

I've already referred to the importance of positivity as an attitude that is conducive to creativity. If our emotional state is in negativity mode, we will not be receptive to new ideas and opportunities. James Brook, Director of Strengths Partnership writes about these two paths, which he calls the path of possibility versus the path of limitation. Negative thinking leads to the latter, whereas a positive mindset leads to an openness to possibility.

Mind space or having a clear space for thinking/reflecting is also important. If my head is full of thoughts, cluttered with to do lists, concerns etc. there's no space for allowing my unconscious to develop ideas. They just get drowned out! Meditation, for example, can help create this space as can taking time out in an inspirational peaceful surrounding.

## 4.4 Risk

Risk is an interesting influencer on creative behaviours. There are many considerations for how much risk is acceptable. For example, if there are physical safety considerations, there will be boundaries to new ideas to ensure that safety requirements are met. The level of resources also has an impact. Limited resources for exploring new options will possibly (but not always) limit a team's level of initiative for new approaches. This comment from a person in an engineering role highlights these points:

> *To be honest, if we get some other solutions ... more practical more widely used maybe I would go for the other way. Because it is more reliable ... already it has been tested by many people ... by many engineers ... it is a more reliable way. So of course I am not going to say no for a wild idea but it depends on if it is a really good idea and we can think about it and in some cases it might*

*be ... you need a lot of things to support it. So in our case we don't have those kinds of resources. So we cannot prove that it works. So my attitude would be to say no. Lim*

Employees will also be sensitive to the organisation's cultural attitude to risk. If people are 'punished' for trying something new and then failing at it, new ways of doing things will not be explored.

**Think about your approach to risk and the company's organisational culture.**
Earlier we looked at diversity: an interesting issue around differences, particularly cultural differences, is attitude to risk. Is diversity enabling risk or limiting it? It has been shown that some cultures are more risk averse than others, as are some organisations. One of our interviewees observed that in Asia if you show an error or a problem, you are held accountable for it.

As a result, creating a culture tolerant of failure can be difficult in Asia. The effects of risk aversion are that there will be less openness to experiment and acceptance of new ideas. For an environment of openness and acceptance of learning, mistakes need to be allowable, within reason of course, while risk aversion would be a counter factor to this.

**Differing viewpoints on risk**
Tracy and I have different perspectives on risk. This is another area where we explored our differences in ideas. And again a snippet from this conversation.

**Tracy** Risk is an interesting influencer on creative behaviours. How much risk is acceptable must be considered. The risks around physical safety, availability of resources, or cultural conditions can all impose boundaries to creative problem solving.

**Barbara** I can accept that boundaries have to be put in place at times when working creatively. However, an openness to risk is important and this of course must be appropriate to the situation. Engineers will be more creative and come up with new ideas at the beginning of projects, but will limit the risk later on in the project. Risk is about being willing to fail – there's a time for risk and a time when it's not appropriate.

## 4.5 Where do new ideas come from?

New ideas can pop into your head anywhere and at any time. Perhaps when you're on your own, when you're discussing an idea with a colleague, or in a boisterous team meeting. Leaders encourage the best conditions for creative thinking in each environment. For example, ensure your team members have time and a quiet space for reflection and analysis. Encourage a culture where people regularly run ideas by each other in one-to-one discussions. Team meetings can also lead to rich discussions if they are managed in a way which encourages sharing of ideas. You'll recognise that some people are more suited to one environment than another, so provide the opportunity that meets their preferred learning style. As we discuss throughout this book, you will need to ensure that there is both time and trust for creative ideas to emerge.

Ideas can also come from the physical external environment:

> *Everywhere. My ideas come from sitting on the train station – or while thinking about a job that I am doing … A lot has to be from the media. When I am shopping – everything. I get my ideas visually. Liam*

Ideas can also come from internal sources. You need to be attuned to these:

> *I guess that it is a mix of everything. It depends if it has come up in a newsfeed or from different things like that, externally from different sites and things that we subscribe to. … Something will come in and we will go - that's a really good idea. … It could be – an idea from a magazine subscription – it is not just online … people going to conferences and hearing things and coming back. Sally*

Ideas can come from many sources. Be aware of this, but more importantly when you 'catch' something that you think will be useful, take a photo of it or jot it down so you can revisit the idea later. As we mention many times, your unconscious mind will continue to think about it.

## 4.6 Virtual teams

Technology and globalisation have changed the workplace. The globalisation of business and the internet have made remote working a reality for many. People work in airports, planes, coffee shops and at home. According to an article in *The New York Times* 43 per cent of employed Americans said they spent at least some time working remotely. Additionally, many employees have team members who are physically separated from them.

If you manage a team where some or all are remote, you need to be even more conscious of the need to include everyone in the discussion and idea generation process. It's not as easy when you are not all physically together. Elements of communication can be lost, as you can see in Figure 5 which was developed by Meridian Resource Associates (MRA). For example, we can see that face-to-face, person-to-person communication has all the elements that facilitate good communication: words used, control over format, voice tone, immediate feedback, non-verbal actions, aspects of the physical environment, physical exchange and informal exchange. At the other end of the scale, email only has words. So be aware of what might be lost in communication when the team is not physically present together.

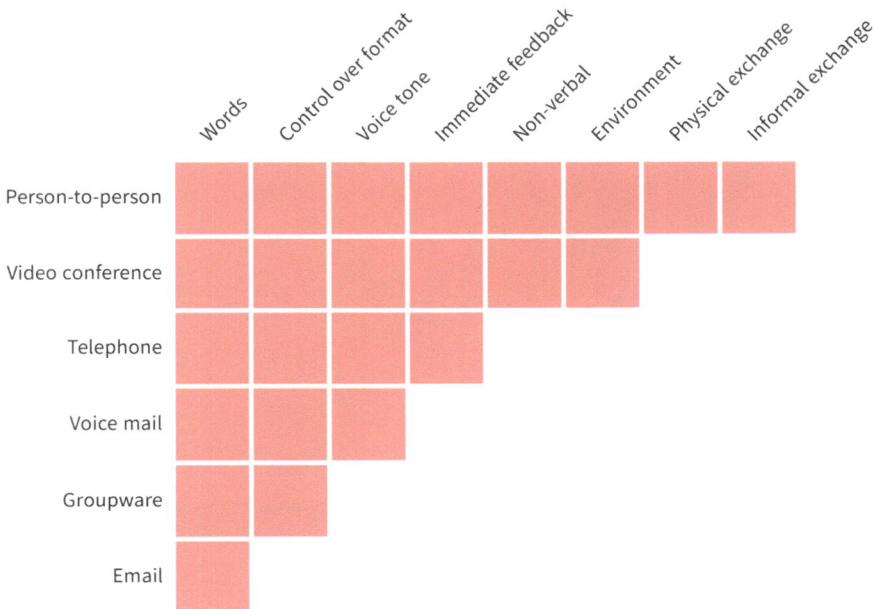

**Figure 5** Communicating Across Technologies – MRA (1997)

## 4.7 Assessing your team's creative climate

*Are you interested in measuring your team's proclivity to creativity? Barbara and I are both fans of the Situational Outlook Questionnaire* which discerns climates that encourage or discourage creativity. The tool is based on the original work of Goran Ekvall and considers:

- Challenge
- Freedom
- Idea time
- Dynamism
- Idea support
- Trust and openness
- Playfulness
- Conflicts
- Debates
- Risk-taking

More information on these attributes can be found in the Appendix and below, along with a link to the tool. http://www.soqonline.net/

## 4.8 Takeaways: Building a creative team environment

- Create an environment where people feel safe to explore different ideas and approaches.

- Collaboration is king for creativity. Encourage collaboration within and across teams.

- You're a role model. Your team will take their cues from you. If you are open to new ways of doing things, they may follow.

- Diversity of background in team members supports diversity of perspective.

- Change your physical space to support change in the thinking.

**REFLECTION POINTS**

**If your team is physically dispersed what steps can you take to develop a creative environment?**

**How will you allow for differences in styles and roles to be respected?**

# Part 5
# Being creative: Tools and practices for creative problem solving

Hopefully, you will now have reflected upon the individual conditions for encouraging creativity and the importance of a suitable team environment. In this part we want to introduce you to the third major strand of our journey towards a more creative workplace.

This section provides practical tools, practices and processes for encouraging creativity. Many of these are based on the structured Creative Problem Solving process originally devised by Sid Parnes in the 1950s, and later developed by Alex Osborne. VanGundy has used this as a basis for his extensive overview of both the CPS process and range of techniques which can be used in Creative Problem Solving. Barbara speaking here, the main part of this section is based upon work I have done over the years since I first encountered creative problem solving on the Open University MBA.

## 5.1 What is Creative Problem Solving (CPS)?

I would like to introduce to you an approach to solving problems which offers a complete cycle, from identifying the problem to implementing it. However, before we do, we would also confirm our belief that this methodology can be undertaken with limited resources.

The process can be done in one session of around six hours or over a period of time, allowing small amounts of quality time to work on it, followed by incubation time when you and the team can get on with your day job. We will show you how this can be done, and with little need for expensive tools.

Creative Problem Solving is an approach that makes use of cycles of divergent and convergent techniques so that there is challenge at each stage of the process to open up to new ways of seeing and thinking. **The three-stage approach**, which is based upon the work of Osborne and Parnes, starts by exploring the problem, then looking for solutions and finally working on implementation.

For this form of problem solving to be effective, certain fundamental requirements must be met.

- **CPS requires an open, positive approach.** We all make assumptions and build up mindsets based upon these. It's important in seeing things differently that these assumptions are challenged. Negativity in this process can be harmful and can shut ideas down. 'Yes, and …' is a useful phrase here rather than 'yes, but …'

- **CPS works best when more time is spent on the early stages of exploring the problem**. What we assume to be the problem may not be the real problem but based upon assumptions that could be challenged. It may be possible to reframe the problem, and by doing so, change the nature of the problem, or even see it disappear!

- **CPS works best when people are being playful** and experimenting with new ideas. This, for me, means taking it out of the boardroom, away from desks and chairs!

- **CPS works best with a group of people from diverse backgrounds** as this can be very helpful in creating the challenging atmosphere that CPS needs.

- **CPS takes time**. However, I would argue that we often address problems by assuming we understand them and then immediately looking for solutions. This means that we spend endless time on solutions that don't work, and by trying to solve the wrong problem.

You may ask, 'Why is this different to non-creative problem solving?'

Well, to start with, the process requires a longer period exploring what the problem actually is. How many times do we assume we know what the problem is, then leap to solutions? You must be familiar with situations where it's been said: 'we have a problem, it's this, what shall we do about it?' The problem here is that often we don't know what exactly the problem is, especially if it's a messy problem or wicked problem. Problems often exist in a hierarchy and we may be looking at a lower order problem rather than the higher overarching problem.

Once the problem is explored in order to see the real problem underlying it, the process can move onto looking for ideas for solutions.

## 5.2 Wicked or complex problems

If you have a problem that requires you to decide between two alternatives, perhaps new logo designs or product features, it's probably not a wicked problem and doesn't require creative problem solving. However, often the problems we struggle with have many features to them and it's this which makes them so difficult to solve. It's for these problems that creative problem solving is designed.

Several researchers and writers have come up with frameworks for deciding if a problem is sufficiently wicked; I've simplified the criteria cited by Mason and Mitroff for you here.

Wicked, or messy, complex problems share these characteristics:

- They are interconnected with other complex problems and complicated in terms of the relationships around the problem.
- They exist in an uncertain environment.
- They display ambiguity because they can be interpreted in many different ways, and this ambiguity is or can lead to conflict.
- The solving of complex problems will involve social, organisational and political as well as technological constraints.

'How to resolve climate change' is a classic example of a wicked problem.

## 5.3 Divergent and convergent phases

Cycling through the stages of a Creative Problem Solving process requires periods of both divergent and convergent thinking.

In the divergent phases, it's crucial that all possibilities are considered and even the wildest of ideas are noted. There is no judgement or censoring in these phases.

Once sufficient time has been allowed for the divergent phase – that is when the objective of the phase has been achieved – the process moves on to the convergent phase.

It's important to keep the process open until all three stages have been completed: exploring the problem; generating ideas; implementing the solution.

Figure 6 illustrates the three stages of the CPS process with their divergent and convergent phases.

**STAGE 1  EXPLORE PROBLEM**

**OPEN UP**
DIVERGE

**Explore different angles of the problem**
An understanding of the 'issue' is achieved

**CLOSE DOWN**
CONVERGE

**Select key problem to work with**
Frame the problem

**STAGE 2  GENERATE IDEAS AND PLANS**

**OPEN
UP**

**Generate ideas to solve the problem**
Many possible solutions/actions have been noted

**CLOSE
DOWN**

**Select preferred options**
Preferred solution(s) selected

**STAGE 3  IMPLEMENT PLAN**

**OPEN
UP**

**Review implementation issues and bullet-proof the plans**
Possible barriers to implementation identified

**CLOSE
DOWN**

**Develop action plans**
Agreed actions for implementation

**Figure 6** Overview of Convergent and Divergent phases

## Creative techniques for addressing wicked problems

Let's now look at a range of techniques you can use in the CPS process with guidelines around how to use them.

This is not prescriptive. Some techniques can be used at different stages, and there are many other techniques which can be used. We have chosen to present only those techniques that we have facilitated.

When describing each technique, we allocate them to a category of either image or word-based tools. Each of these has its merits, and its difficulties, and we provide an overview of these.

This table, Figure 7, supplements Figure 6 above with our suggested techniques at each stage of the CPS process.

**STAGE 1 EXPLORE PROBLEM**

DIVERGE

Rich pictures, Collage, Visioning, Metaphor,
Ask why? Fishbone diagram

CONVERGE

Reframing the 'issue'

**STAGE 2 GENERATE IDEAS AND PLANS**

DIVERGE

Classic brainstorming, Brainwriting, Negative brainstorming
and reversals, Superheroes, Random stimuli

CONVERGE

Sticky dots, Cartoon storyboard

**STAGE 3  IMPLEMENT PLAN**

DIVERGE

Force field analysis, Help Hinder,
Disney technique

CONVERGE

Cartoon storyboard, Action plan

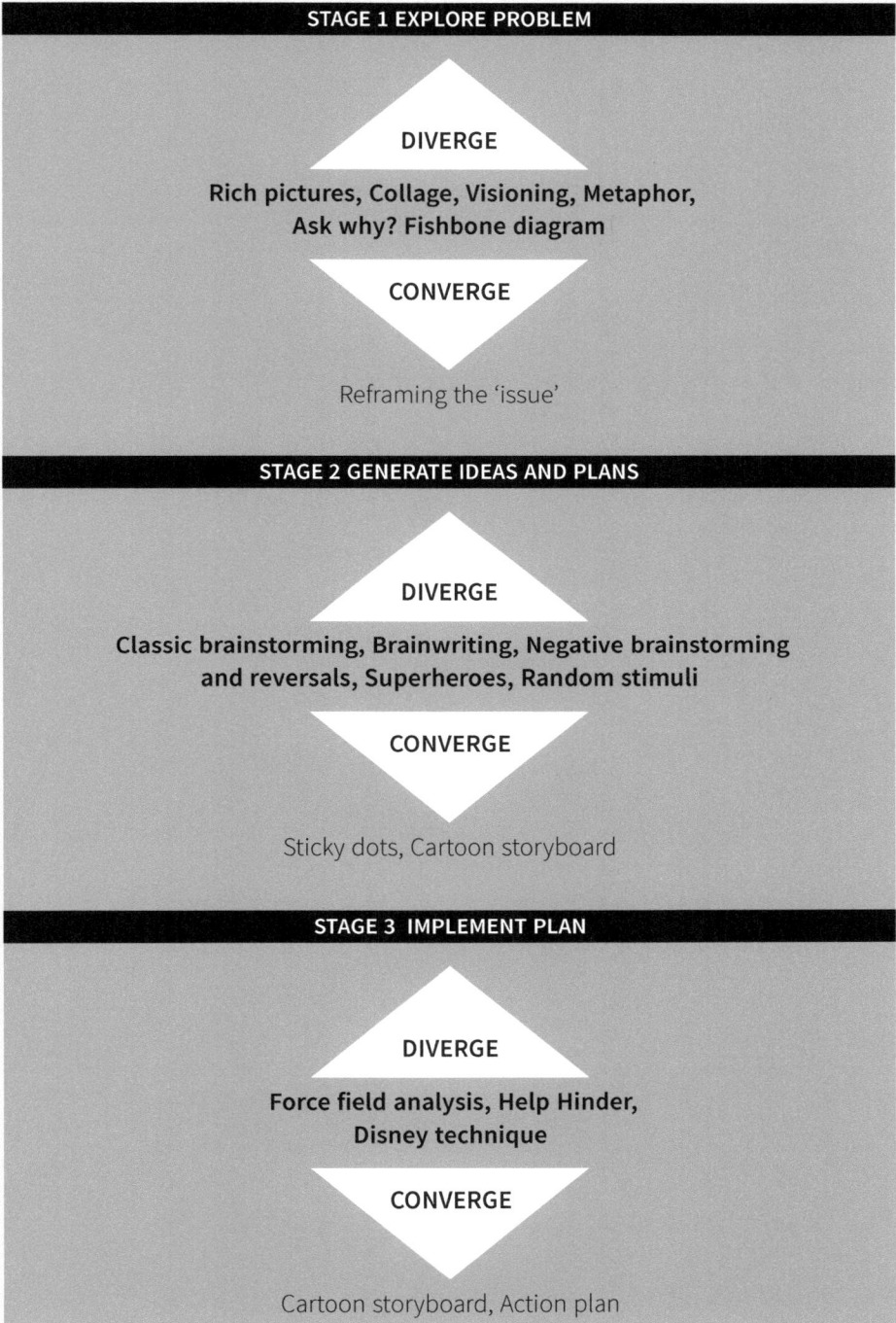

**Figure 7** Tools best suited to each stage

## 5.4 Image and word-based tools

**Image-based tools**

Using imagery as a creative tool takes us out of our normal established way of working, with words, and creates conditions for our intuition to come into play. We capture intuitive reactions that cannot yet be put into the 'right' words and which are not yet consciously realised. These can be thoughts, emotions and values which have often not been expressed consciously. These add a richness to our exploration and can surprise us with their result.

Image-based tools focus on using imagery to better understand the problem. Imagery addresses a different part of the brain and allows the unconscious or intuition to work more than the logical rational part of the brain.

Intuition is valuable in breaking through into new ways of thinking. I would always recommend beginning with image-based tools because:

- They can signal to participants that this is different from the normal discussion-based work.

- They allow perceptions, which are subjective, to show through. This is particularly valuable when there is ambiguity in the problem.

- They are less censured than words and can allow for more open ideas.

- They are more fun and allow a sense of play at the beginning, which is needed when working creatively.

**Word-based tools**

Working with words can result in a tendency to remain on the logical/rational spectrum of thinking. As words are more precise, and need less interpretation, word-based tools can be carried out in shorter time-frames. This can be more acceptable in many settings. However, words can also be a barrier for people whose native language is different.

The choice of whether to use image-based or word-based tools will be influenced by:

- Your own style preference and comfort level as a facilitator
- The acceptability of tools for the team
- The objective of the exercise at the time
- The stage of the CPS process.

During the CPS process, image-based tools work well initially to open up the minds of participants to new ways of thinking. Once this happens, word-based tools will allow this openness to continue.

**Combination tools**

Some techniques and processes employ both a visual element as well as being word-based. We'll look at one example, Edward de Bono's Six Thinking Hats where a team is asked to metaphorically put on a hat and view a situation or problem through a single perspective. You may also find that use of metaphor, cartoon storyboard and superheroes will come into this category.

What's important here is to reflect upon the value of going beyond words in creative techniques and using imagery to help the unconscious and intuition come into play.

# 5.5 Creative techniques for the CPS process

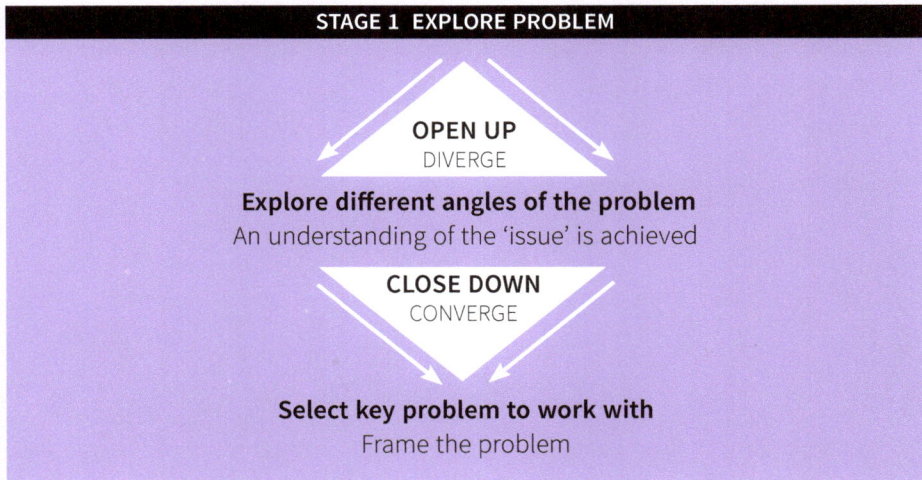

**STAGE 1 EXPLORE PROBLEM**

**OPEN UP**
DIVERGE

**Explore different angles of the problem**
An understanding of the 'issue' is achieved

**CLOSE DOWN**
CONVERGE

**Select key problem to work with**
Frame the problem

This stage revolves around a range of techniques to enable a broad understanding of the problem. It's important to involve as many people and perspectives as possible and also to incorporate some aspect of **Fresh-Eye** as described in Part 3.

# Techniques to use at the *Explore Problem* stage of the CPS process

## Divergent Phase

# Rich Picture (opposite)

### Description

This is one of several image-based techniques that are very helpful in the early stages of problem exploration. Using imagery can allow more of the nuances, and the tacit knowledge to emerge around a problem. It can help us understand the elements of a problem better than using words.

A Rich Picture is a pictorial map of the problem, showing its elements and relationships between them. It's a bit like a mind map with pictures and connections used instead of words. This connection element is important to highlight complexities.

### The picture can be produced in several ways:

- As a team effort, at the beginning of the exploration stage of the CPS process, to gain an understanding of the problem.

- As an individual exercise to allow differing perceptions of the problem to arise.

- When not all those present are so familiar with all the elements of the problem, it can be done in pairs. Pairing up someone who is very familiar with someone less so can be valuable. The picture can be drawn by the person with more experience, with the second person acting as a coach and asking questions to gain more insight and help the picture creation process. Equally it could be done the other way around with the person with experience describing and their partner drawing.

# Climate Change

## The choice of which way to facilitate this activity will depend upon several factors:

- The competence of individual team members to produce a picture. While it does not require a high level of skill, it does require a good knowledge of the problem and its elements.

- The complexity of the problem, and whether it's possible to produce a joint picture.

- Your facilitation skills, for example in handling the emergence of many differing perceptions. If this happens, you'd need to be able to handle it.

### Resources needed

- Large pieces of paper and coloured pens
- Somewhere to pin or tape the picture when finished.

### How to facilitate

Explain the purpose of the activity and allow a suitable amount of time to complete, maybe 20 to 30 minutes. Then step back and only intervene to answer questions about the process. Once completed, ask for an explanation of the picture, then ask for insights from everyone present, making sure these insights are captured. Ideally the picture will throw up more insights around the problem.

Summarised below are benefits and considerations for using Rich Picture

| TABLE 3  BENEFITS AND CONSIDERATIONS OF RICH PICTURE | |
| --- | --- |
| **Benefits** | **Considerations** |
| All elements of a complex problem are uncovered early on. | Can be difficult at first if participants don't like drawing. |
| It brings out tacit knowledge. | If the results show widely differing perceptions, it will take time to work through the differences. |
| The emergence of differing perceptions is valuable early in the process. | |

# Collage

### Description
This can be an alternative to drawing a Rich Picture to express the problem.

The picture, Figure 8, below shows a collage produced at a recent workshop facilitated by Barbara.

**Figure 8** Illustration of Collage

### How to use
With this exercise each participant puts together a collage of pictures, to which they can add drawing but no words, to represent their perception of the problem. It's advisable here to have each person produce their own collage.

As with the Rich Picture, the process requires time to complete and careful facilitation to unearth the assumptions and perceptions.

## It's helpful because:

- It takes away the pressure of drawing pictures.
- It taps into the intuitive, creative part of the brain and can unlock unconscious thoughts.
- It's fun and playful, which is important for creativity.
- It provides a tangible expression of a vision, which can then be discussed and worked around.
- It stimulates the use of metaphor and analogy.
- It can be interpreted differently by different people and allows feelings and perspectives to emerge.
- It challenges assumptions about your world.

It's a very powerful tool and, as it can reveal issues that were previously unconscious, it needs to be handled sensitively. It can also continue providing insights after the workshop.

## Resources needed

- A supply of pre-cut pictures from magazines, or magazines from which participants can cut out their pictures (I like to have a selection of pictures ready in advance as it takes less time than searching though magazines).
- Large sheet of paper for each person.
- Scissors and glue stick to stick the pictures on the paper.
- Tape to put the final pictures on the wall.

## Facilitation

- The resources need to be placed on tables around the room, or centrally, so that participants can walk around them.

- Try using quiet music in the background and discourage discussion during the process. Laughter is encouraged!

- Participants are given a specific amount of time to collect images and make their collage. Encourage intuitive choice, without too much thought, of pictures to represent the purpose of the process.

- As this process can be used both in creating a future vision, and in describing the current state, instructions will obviously vary. For visioning instructions, see the section on visioning.

- After the allocated amount of time, either you can ask each person to present their collage to others, or they can share in pairs. When sharing, ask others not to ask questions, just to note their insights.
- Often the best way is to have a gallery of collages, and everyone views them and adds their insights. This can be done by adding post-its to the image.

- At the end of the process, each participant collects the insights.

As this is an individual exercise, the next stage is to work on a combined collage to take into account all the differing perceptions and insights. This is not an easy exercise. Perhaps combine those that deal with similar perceptions and then capture differences on a separate piece of paper that can be reviewed later.

Messy problems often involve messiness in the process. What is important is that all perceptions are valid and none should be negated at this exploration stage. Again, we've summarised a few things to think about when deciding whether to use collage.

### TABLE 4  BENEFITS AND CONSIDERATIONS OF COLLAGE

| Benefits | Considerations |
| --- | --- |
| This can be a fun activity and can raise the energy level in the room. | It's not so implicit as a Rich Picture and will need more careful interpretation. |
| It's more appealing to people who don't like drawing. | It takes time to prepare the resources and to clear away. |
| The technique can also be used to create a vision for the future. | |

# Creating a shared vision

Creating a vision is essential in any change process. A vision offers us a strong mental image of something we want to create in the future and it can motivate us towards that future. When the vision involves others, engaging them in a shared vision is extremely valuable. It's particularly powerful and inspiring if it's developed as an **image** rather than using words, and can inspire people to work collaboratively with leaders and engage in their future.

In the Creative Problem Solving process a vision can be created in the initial divergent stage around understanding the problem. Its purpose is to take participants into a future where the problem has already been solved.

In this section, after introducing the overall concept, we offer a variety of ways in which visioning can be facilitated. Some of them are Barbara's favourites and some Tracy's.  Experiment with these different approaches.

Before working to understand the current situation, ask participants to envision what it would look like in a future state when the problem is solved. Not all problems lend themselves to this tool, however when they do, it becomes very powerful.

**Barbara:** I was inspired to use visioning in my creativity workshops after encountering the work of **Marjorie Parker** with the Norwegian company, Hydro Aluminium. For me, this was such a powerful example of creating a vision that worked in very practical terms that I wanted to share it with you here.

In the 1980s a new Managing Director was appointed to one of the Norwegian plants, Karmoy Fabrikker which was emerging from a period of crisis, and Ms Parker was invited in to work with him. As a result of early discussions, a vision was created for a future state of Karmoy. This was based around a garden metaphor that was drawn up by a local artist and then presented to the workforce to inspire them to design their interpretation of the vision for their parts of the organisation.

As a practical measure of the success of the whole exercise, there was a recorded increase in productivity of 33% over a three-year period when the process was developing, and in addition, safety increased and environmental emissions decreased.

So, what are the lessons that can be taken from this example?
Of the many reflections Marjorie Parker included in the book Creating Shared Vision here are several that I want to share with you.

Initially, it was assumed that in the company, employees are responsible people, have a desire to make a difference, and that the employer has an obligation to ensure that employees reach their potential.

There was an attitude that a long-term approach to competitive advantage was needed.

Visioning opened up possibilities for all employees within Karmoy to have clear direction and to have permission to discuss the future and how best to organise their work.

Employees have taken the opportunity to develop their ideas and it has opened up their creativity.

# Image-based visioning

**Following are guidelines on how to start.**

**In introducing the concept of visioning, explain what it is, and why you are facilitating it at this stage of the process.**

1. Start by ensuring that everyone is relaxed and has paper and pens to hand for drawing. At this stage some quiet meditative music can help create a calm state of mind.

2. Encourage participants to sit comfortably with legs uncrossed. If it's suitable they could lie on a carpet.

3. Take participants through a relaxation exercise if you feel confident about doing it. Some participants may feel uncomfortable at first, however it's very useful for clearing the mind and allowing the imagery to happen.

4. Spend a short amount of time, around 5 minutes to encourage participants to relax by flexing and relaxing muscles in turn. Start first with their feet, then move to legs, thighs, buttocks, stomach, chest, arms, shoulders, and finally face.

5. Then ask participants to visualise a familiar object such as an apple, or orange. This leads them into being able to conjure up an image and its associated senses.

6. Then ask people to imagine a future when 'the problem' is resolved, what will it look like, what will be happening, who will be there, what can they feel, smell etc. Encourage them to sense fully this future state.

7. The relaxation and imaging instructions can take about 10 minutes. Then allow time for people to create the image in their mind.

8. After about 5 minutes ask them to draw, or paint, or make a collage to represent this future. Please note that if you have used collage earlier, use drawing or painting here instead.

9. When everyone has completed their vision, suggest they share in pairs first, then each pair to join up with another one and again share. Ask them to consider what came up for them from this picture. Ask that insights are captured from this sharing in an appropriate way.

10. Finally, share in a gallery style so everyone can see the visions created. It may be important here for the whole group to draw up a common image, as described in the collage technique. Ensure that in creating one collage, no important messages are lost.

11. One way of creating a common team vision is for the small groups to work on combining their visions. If the team is relatively small, no more than twelve, you'll only have three variations to work with.

# Role play and other variations on Visioning

### Description
Some people love to act. (Typically the extroverts!). Alongside imagery and collage, role play can also be an interesting way to imagine a new future and have fun. This process involves developing a short role play where preferably everyone has a part.

### How to use
The team can choose a big picture future and/ or one aspect of a future vision, such as say customer experience, that they will represent through the role play.

- Encourage the teams to keep the role play simple in concept.

- As Barbara suggested earlier, participants start by using their intuition to develop an image or concept of the future without prior discussion.

- They then share this with the team and discuss which parts will be used for the role play and how these could be presented.

- Assign roles. Prepare and practice the role play.

- Each team presents their story/role play in no more than ten minutes.

- Allow time at the end of the presentation for questions and discussion.

### Resources needed
Quiet space for each team with room to prepare for the role play.
Theatre style space where teams can present
Paper and pens.
Camera/Video.

My experience is that teams often seek out other props and are resourceful in finding them.

# Painting the future

### Description
Another visual exercise using paint and canvases. When I've facilitated this activity, the outcome was a large painting by the team with several representations of a future. The activity could also be done individually. There are pros and cons to each approach.

### How to use
This is part of the problem exploration stage of the CPS or another process such as the Six Thinking Hats method.

The next step would be to take that problem and imagine that all the barriers had been overcome and that the perfect result had been realised.

If it's a team effort, as above, allow time for the team to brainstorm and plan what the painting would look like, and then time to paint it.

A spokesperson (or two) from the team then explains the meaning of the painting. Time depends upon the number of teams. Each team should have five minutes to present and five minutes to answer questions.

People can amaze you when they are given permission to represent their ideas creatively.

### Resources needed
One large canvas. Encourage the teams to paint on the same canvas (my preference), although you can provide one canvas per team (or one canvas per participant).
Paint
Paint trays – several per team
Easel to hold canvas
Paint brushes
Ground sheets if painting inside (very important)
Camera/Video
Participants to bring old shirts/clothes to protect their clothing

# Metaphor and Visioning

### Description

A metaphor is a figure of speech in which an image is used to denote something else in order to better understand it, for example, the common metaphor for an organisation as a machine. Gareth Morgan in his book *Imaginization* introduces the concept of using metaphors as a creative tool to change how we think about things.

In the CPS process, we can use metaphors in the first stage to understand the problem better.

For example, teams have used a metaphor of a slow oil tanker to express how the department or organisation is working. Once the metaphor is expressed, and drawn, it provides insights into other aspects of the problem which can then be captured in a brainstorm.

Visioning can also make use of metaphor as in the example of the vision for Karmoy which was drawn as a flourishing garden. The discussion can then be around what this means for the organisation, taking the components of the metaphor and breaking them down.

We can also use metaphor for reframing a problem. For example, if we see the organisation as a machine, what would happen if we reframe it as a fast sports car? What would the difference be? This opens the possibility to new thinking. This approach can be used to explore how things are now compared to a desirable new future.

Be aware that metaphors can create a rigid way of thinking as much as opening new ideas, because metaphor frames our thoughts. When we use the machine metaphor for organisations we start to use words that fit this, for example, well-oiled machine, mechanics, structure, all of which can prevent us from opening to new more flexible possibilities.

### Using metaphor to create a vision

Sometimes it can feel threatening to ask participants to develop an image, or paint or sculpt something. Using metaphor can be a less threatening way of exploring a future ideal situation.

It's useful to start the activity as an individual exercise and afterwards work to combine the metaphors.

To begin, ask participants to take a large piece of paper, then guide them through a relaxation and visioning exercise where they imagine a future state in which the problem has been resolved.

Then ask them to draw a metaphor to represent this future state.

Collage can also be used to create a vision. By doing so, it allows participants to create a vision in a less threatening way than drawing it.

**Feedback on vision created**

The results of all vision-creating exercises need to be explored, so that they can be considered in the subsequent stage of the CPS process.

When visioning is done within this process, it's important to accept that these are the ideas of the team or the individual, rather than to have a general discussion about the ideas. At this stage it's not necessary to determine which is the 'correct' vision. They are all relevant perspectives.

This is different from the process of creating a shared vision in a strategy/values/ vision session or even a team building session.

To achieve this level of acceptance, I would normally ask for insights rather than feedback. An effective way is to present the images in a gallery around the room, then ask participants to add their insights onto each one. This again taps into the intuition and can be very helpful. The original presenter(s) of the vision collects the insights and any further feedback and can take this into consideration by editing their vision. At this stage they may also choose to just note the insights.

Using the insights as a resource for establishing what the problem is completes the first stage of the CPS process, Explore the Problem. Brainstorming the gap between the current situation and the future vision is a possible method to begin stage 2, Generate Ideas. Combining this with the Storyboard approach is particularly powerful.

As we have suggested several times here that visioning can be done as an individual or a team effort Table 5 may be helpful in deciding on approach. This would apply whether painting, drawing or developing a vision through another medium such as collage.

| TABLE 5 BENEFITS AND CONSIDERATIONS OF TEAM VERSUS INDIVIDUAL VISIONING | | |
|---|---|---|
| | **Benefits** | **Considerations** |
| **Team** | If the vision is shared before drawing up the image (in whichever format chosen), this can lead to a healthy discussion. | Some participants may not feel as involved as others if it is left to only 1 or 2 people. |
| | Can have a stronger team building effect. | Discussion before capturing the vision becomes planning and can lead to a more rational approach, missing out the intuitive advantages of visioning. |
| | Can allow those who feel uncomfortable with painting etc, to contribute ideas. | |
| **Individual** | Everyone has the opportunity to participate. | People may feel awkward if they feel they lack painting or other creative skills. |
| | It allows for different perspectives to be shared. | Drawing up a team vision may become more difficult if there are wide variations of individual visions. |

# Ask Why?

A simple and powerful tool for exploring problems which can also be combined with other tools in the CPS process is asking **Why?**

The problem owner, or someone they've designated because they know all or most elements of the problem, is questioned by others in the group only asking 'why?' Each use of 'why?' delves further into the problem, digging for deeper understanding. It's recommended to use this at least five times.

Facilitating is important here as this should not develop into a general discussion, nor should judgements be made. Only the one word 'why?' and the answers which are captured on flip chart, or similar.

The aim is to build an understanding of the complexity of the problem, which could then be captured in a rich picture.

# Fishbone Diagram

**Description**

This tool was developed by Professor Kaoru Ishikawa and is sometimes referred to as an Ishikawa diagram.

**How to use**

The process involves drawing a fishbone diagram with the main bones representing the problem to be explored. Out of this, other bones are drawn to show the main contributing factors to the problem, and then smaller bones coming off these. It's a bit like a mind map of causes of the problem, and provides a more structured approach than a Rich Picture.

The main causes can be highlighted, which could be used for determining a boundary over which aspect of the problem will be addressed first when dealing with a complicated multi-layered problem. The Figure 9 below shows an example of the type of structure you might have for the Fishbone.

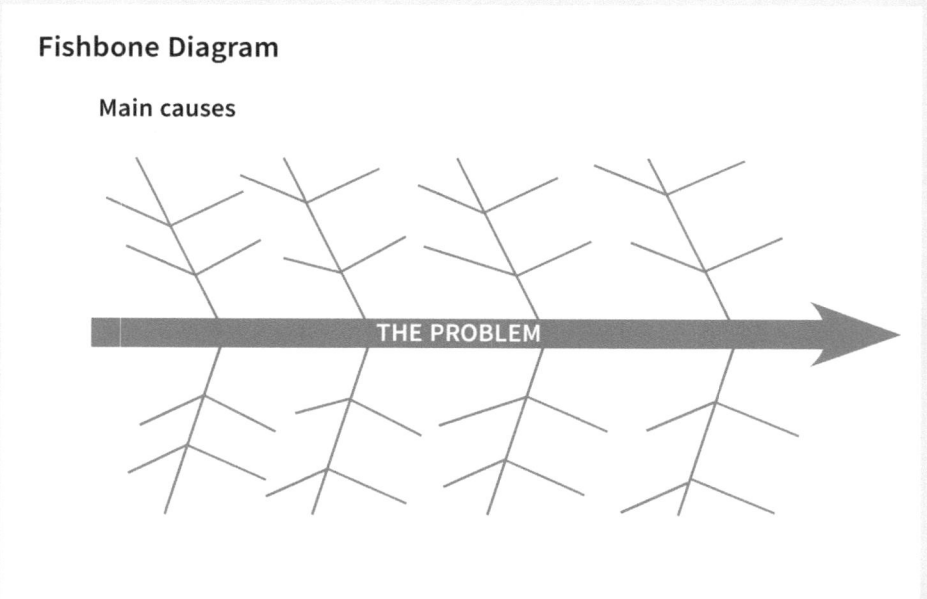

**Fishbone Diagram**

Main causes

THE PROBLEM

**Figure 9** A model fishbone diagram for completion

The fishbone diagram is a simple and logical process for breaking a problem down into its main components.

It enables all aspects of a problem to be identified in order to fully understand the problem.

It helps to show the interconnectedness of parts of a problem.

It prevents an over-emphasis on any one aspect of the problem.

The structured nature of this tool will suit participants who are more logical thinkers. As a word-based tool, it can complement or even summarise an image-based tool such as a Rich Picture.

# Convergent Phase

By now, you should now have a broad understanding of the problem and its complexities.

You may need to determine the level at which you resolve the problem if it consists of different levels. Climate change as a complex problem for example could be addressed at the world stage, continent, country, on an organisational basis or at an individual level. The latter is the lowest point in the hierarchy, although it may be more doable in the time frame.

Next, you'll need to frame the problem as a 'how to' statement so that you can start to look for ways to solve it. An example may be:

'How do we address climate change at the individual level so that people change their habits and attitudes to scarce resources?'

At the end of the Problem Exploration stage you should have an understanding of the problem and its complexities, and a problem statement to take into the next stage.

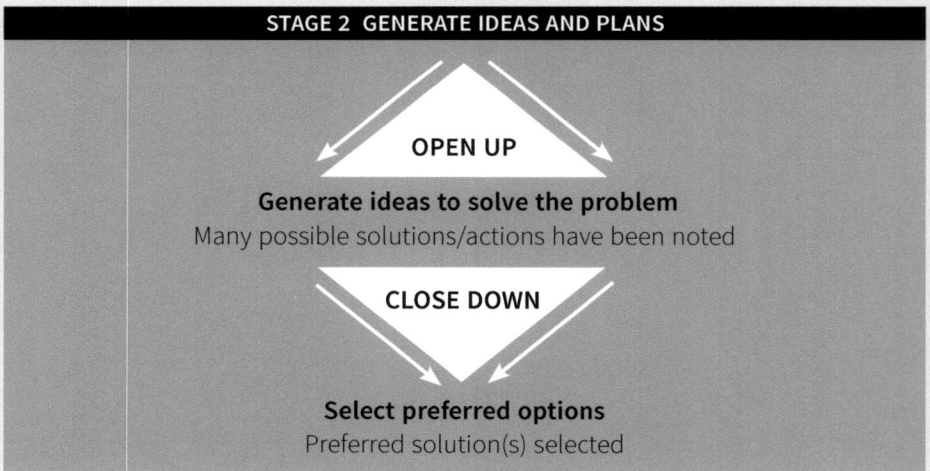

**STAGE 2  GENERATE IDEAS AND PLANS**

**OPEN UP**

**Generate ideas to solve the problem**
Many possible solutions/actions have been noted

**CLOSE DOWN**

**Select preferred options**
Preferred solution(s) selected

The aim of this stage is to generate as many possible ideas for solutions to the problem. The more the better! At the end of the stage, you need to decide whether you are going to choose the best solution or a number of possible solutions.

# Techniques to use at the *Generation of Ideas* stage of CPS

## Divergent Phase

# Brainstorming

This is such an important process. It's used as a basis for many techniques and incorporates a variety of tools within it, as we'll explore later. Let's look first at the diverse types of brainstorming, and then at some of the important takeaways for a leader facilitating a brainstorming session.

Let's start with your experience. I'm certain that you'll have experienced a time when someone has suggested that you all brainstorm a topic. It might be ideas for the next marketing campaign, or ways of handling customer feedback, for example. You may even have initiated this yourself.

It usually goes something like this: 'let's brainstorm' – then you all get together and throw a few ideas out. One of the ideas gets picked up and a discussion follows. During this process you may not have noticed that one of the more introverted members of the team is very quiet. At the end of the 15 minutes allocated, you have a direction to move on. However, are they the best ideas and have all members of the team felt that they have been heard? I'd bet that the answer to these questions is no.

### How can we improve the brainstorming experience?

Brainstorming requires rules if it's to work at its best. In 1963, Osborne proposed some rules that have become invaluable as guidelines for any divergent techniques. Before starting any brainstorming session, it's important that you remind people about these rules, and that, as a facilitator, you enforce them!

- Defer judgement. Do not criticise or even comment on ideas as they are proposed. Any intervention at this stage in the process will end the free thinking and prevent the emergence of unique ideas. The time for judgement will be in the convergent phases.

- Quantity breeds quality. The more ideas generated, the more likelihood of a great idea emerging.

- The wilder the better. Allowing brainstorming to continue and encouraging wild ideas to emerge increases the possibility of that breakthrough thinking. Wild ideas can often be used as a springboard to other ideas.

- Combine and improve ideas. Build upon what others have already noted. Not all ideas generated need to be original, so use ideas already expressed to generate more ideas.

- Take a break from the problem. Switch tools, or try another variation. Take a break and let ideas incubate.

**Varieties of brainstorming**

In all varieties, similar materials are needed:

- Somewhere to capture ideas generated
- Someone to facilitate
- Pens and paper to capture ideas
- Post-it notes. Capture each idea on a post-it, then group the ideas into categories. This makes the following stage easier.

**Here's a summary of the different types of brainstorming sessions.**

- **Classical**. This is where a facilitator, internal or external, notes down ideas on a flip chart as and when they are offered by the members of a team. Ideas can be free flowing from any member or managed by asking each person in turn to come up with an idea.

- **Negative brainstorming**. In this version, team members are asked how they can avoid or stop the problem being solved. This usually generates more fun among teams and can lead to some interesting insights. At the end of this brainstorm, use a reversal exercise to turn each idea around into something positive.

- **Silent brainstorming**. This is often known as brainwriting. Here, team members write ideas on post-its, then put them onto a board. This is a great technique if there are introverts in the team as all members can participate without fear of speaking out. Putting ideas on to post-it notes facilitates the later process of gathering ideas together into themes.

- **Superheroes**. This technique asks participants to take on the characteristics of a one of their heroes, as the title suggests. They then brainstorm as if they are that person. Increase the power of this tool by adding a visual aspect. Ask people to dress and act like their hero: even just adding some aspect of dress such as a cape as if they were to be Batman adds a new dimension – and fun. This tool can be very effective for breakthrough ideas, however it needs careful facilitation, resources for dressing up, and will need a warm-up exercise beforehand.

### Brainstorming in the Problem Exploration phase

Although these tools apply mostly to the Idea Generation phase, some tools in the Problem Exploration phase can make use of brainstorming in a more structured way.

It works well to create an initial Rich Picture, or to generate questions for the Asking Why? technique. In both these techniques, the brainstorm will throw up questions rather than answers.

# Random Stimuli

This is a useful technique to use when participants need to take a break or ideas are running dry. It involves taking an object, word or image and using free association to generate other ideas that may be loosely related. This can be similar to using metaphor in the ways in which a metaphor is explored for ideas which can then be applied to the problem.

One way in which this can be used is to suggest that participants go outside for a walk (which also has the benefits of refreshing their energy), find a random object and bring it back into their group. The group takes each object in turn and brainstorms ideas around how that fits the problem.

For example, someone may come in with a stone, and the stone's associations may be that it's smooth, heavy, a soothing colour etc. These thoughts are then force-fitted to the problem, by asking how could this problem be smoothed out, or could we make it less heavy. This may then lead to new insights. It may not throw up many new ideas, however even one new idea may be valuable at this stage.

## Convergent Phase

At the end of the divergent phase it's important to decide what ideas will be taken forward. There are many logical techniques here that you can use to help selection, particularly if it's a technical problem with tight resource issues.

However, for a wicked problem that involves people, it may be more appropriate to look at other techniques and not to lose any of the wilder ideas too soon. One of the dangers of this phase of CPS is that we look at all ideas and select only those that fit with our current mindsets, whereas the process up to now has been about freeing ourselves from mindsets to find a breakthrough solution!

We are offering two techniques here. The first is almost a process in itself and allows all or most ideas to be retained at this stage, the Cartoon Storyboard. The second is Sticky Dots which allows a choice of several ideas to be selected based upon a voting process.

# The Cartoon Storyboard

I have adapted this technique, originally developed by Jane Henry, as a simple process to capture the current state, the future vision and the journey to get from one to the other. By using drawings, we again allow the possibility for the unconscious to work. A big plus is that images become more inspirational and energising. It has proven to be a very versatile tool to use with both individuals and groups in helping them move forward to solving problems and becoming unstuck when considering their future direction.

To complete the Cartoon Storyboard, you will need a large piece of paper and coloured pens and work through the following stages.

1. Draw six boxes as shown in Figure 10.

2. Work through a visioning exercise as described earlier, and put an image to represent this in box 6.

3. Complete a visual exercise such as a Rich Picture to capture elements of where you are now and put an image to represent this in box 1.

4. Work though the idea generation stage of the CPS process to generate ideas for bridging the gap between the state in box 1 and box 6. Put these ideas on post-its so that they can be moved around before the final picture emerges.

| 1. Here is where we are now | 2. | 3. |
|---|---|---|
| 4. | 5. | 6. Here is our future vision ... |

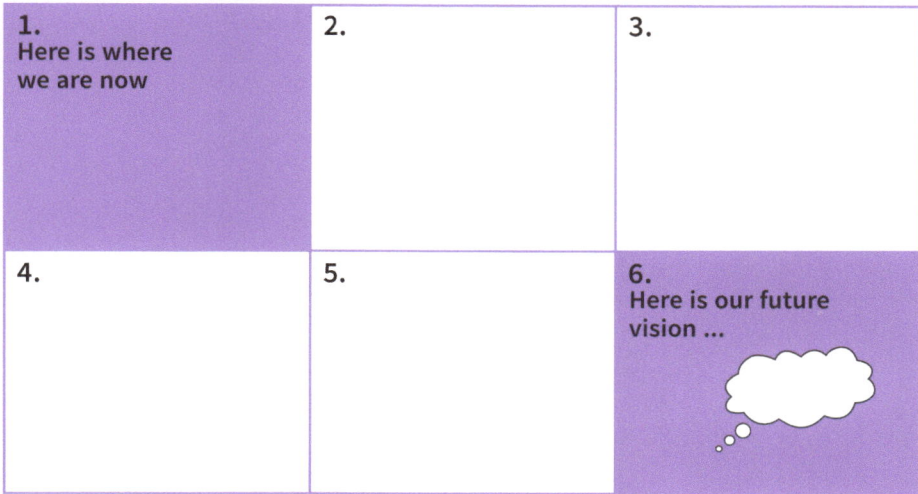

**Figure 10** A model for the Cartoon Storyboard

5. Unlike in CPS idea generation, at this stage all ideas are accepted and the post-its are placed on the storyboard in what seems like a logical flow of ideas.

6. Draw an image in each box from 2 to 5 to represent the selection of ideas posted in it. Do not lose any of the ideas at this stage.

7. Work through the third stage of CPS, looking at what could help/hinder, what the barriers are. Add in actions that may need to be taken for the already chosen ideas to work. Do not discard ideas that seem too wild; look at how they could be reframed, as we saw with the brainstorming tool.

8. Finally, the storyboard can be redrawn, adding any metrics such as times for action completion.

The storyboard can be completed over a period of time or all in one go as a complete exercise. Allow time for both the visioning exercise so that it engages the unconscious, and for the idea generation to allow a good range of ideas to emerge. A storyboard can be completed by a team working on solving a problem or creating a different future, or by an individual working alone or with a mentor or coach.

Figure 11 shows how I combine the CPS process with the Storyboard.

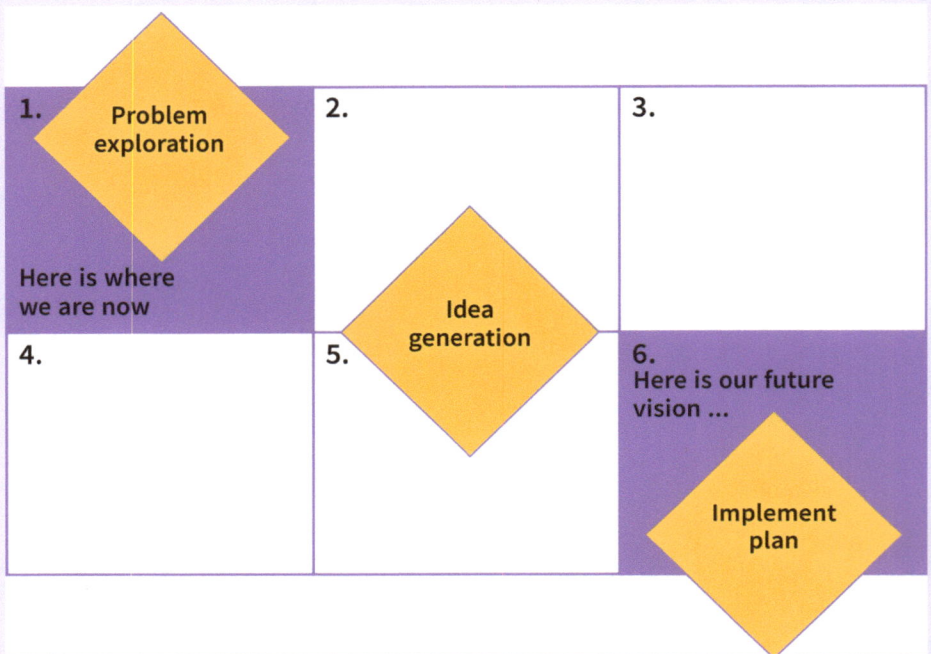

**Figure 11** Combining CPS with the Storyboard (Wilson 2018)

# Sticky Dots

A useful tool for a convergent phase of CPS is called Sticky Dots. It's a silent and visual voting process. Here's how it works.

On a flip chart, list the options that have emerged from the discussion.

Give all team members different coloured sticky dots.

Ask them to select their top two (or three) points.

When the facilitator says GO, everyone places their stickers on the flip chart – without further discussion.

Count the votes for each choice.

Here's an example.

# Sticky Dot

Best options for combating climate change

| Option | Voting |
|---|---|
| Every country achieve 80% target of solar and wind power | |
| Pay climate warming carbon tax unless able to prove zero waste/emission | |
| All petrol and diesel cars replaced by electric cars | |
| Move all properties within 1 kilometer of the coast inland | |

**Figure 12** Example of Sticky Dot voting outcome

There are multiple ways that you can use Sticky Dot voting: for wrapping up a discussion; being efficient with the information; and ensuring everyone's voice is heard.

At the end of the Idea Generation stage you will have either chosen one or more ideas for solutions by selecting form the ideas generated, or captured all or most on the Cartoon Storyboard to work through to an action plan.

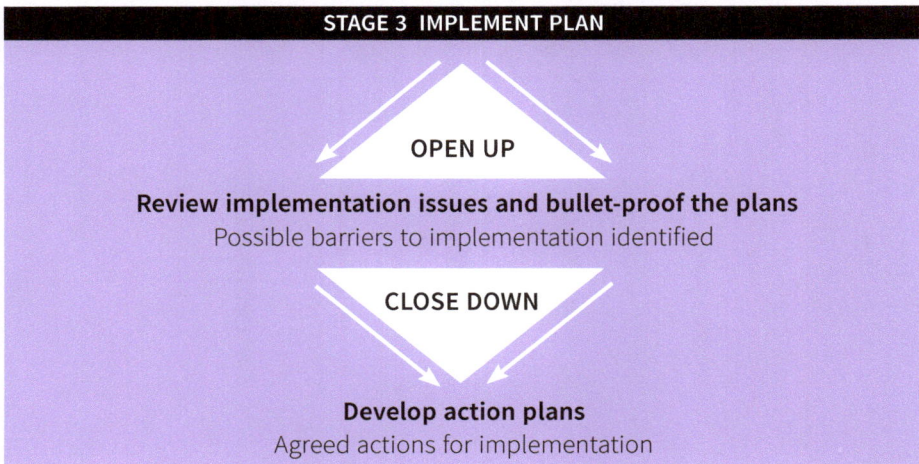

---

**STAGE 3  IMPLEMENT PLAN**

**OPEN UP**

**Review implementation issues and bullet-proof the plans**
Possible barriers to implementation identified

**CLOSE DOWN**

**Develop action plans**
Agreed actions for implementation

# Techniques to use at the *Implementation* stage of CPS

The aim of this stage is to diverge again in order to consider all the issues which could get in the way of the solutions being implemented.

## Divergent Phase

# Force Field Analysis

**Description**
This tool can be very helpful at the implementation phase of the CPS process as it enables an analysis of factors which could prevent the change happening. It also identifies factors which would support the change.

**How to use**
It starts with a brainstorm of all the factors which could either drive the plan forward or restrain the implementation.

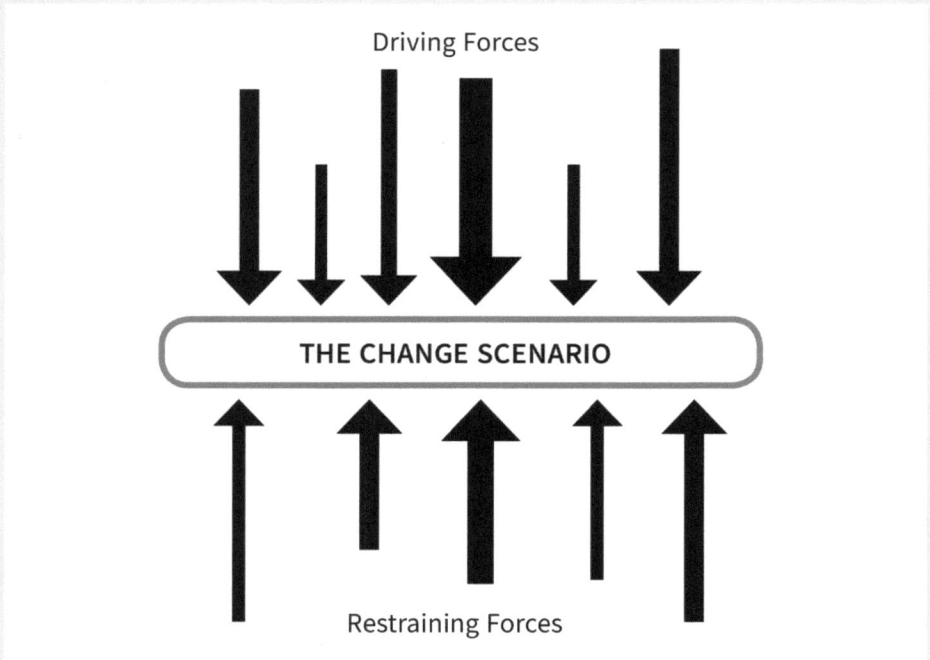

**Figure 13** Force Field analysis – based on work of Kurt Lewin in the 1940s

Identify the relative importance for all factors. Using vertical lines whose thickness represents the relative importance of the factor, draw lines as Figure 13 above shows.

Use the diagram as the basis for further brainstorming around how to avoid or remove the restraining factors. Identify actions to add to the action plan, which you'll develop in the convergent phase.

# Help/Hinder Diagram

### Description
This tool enables you to review all factors that could help or hinder you in the implementation of the planned action. It's therefore a divergent tool in the Implementation phase of CPS.

| TABLE 6 HELP/HINDER DIAGRAM | | |
|---|---|---|
| Factors to consider | Do they help? | Do they hinder? |
| Who? | | |
| What? | | |
| Where? | | |
| When? | | |
| How? | | |

### How to use
As you do with a Force Field Analysis, start with a brainstorm around what factors can help and which ones can hinder. It helps to use the framework of Who, What, Where, When and How to fully explore all the issues. Table 6 gives a structure for the capture of the issues.

It could be that someone or something appears on both sides of the Help/Hinder matrix. For example, a senior manager who is a gatekeeper for the finances needed to support the action plan could be a help if brought onboard, and a hindrance if they are not in agreement. Identifying these factors adds a kind of bullet-proofing to the action plan.

# Disney Technique

### Description
This can be a fun way of looking at the factors that can help or hinder the implementation of a solution.

It's based upon Walt Disney's way of working, and developed into a tool by Robert Dilts, one of the founders of Neuro Linguistic Programming.

It stimulates insights into what barriers there may be to implementation and how to overcome them. This process can be a very valuable way of testing any ideas before presenting them to wider audience. Again, it's a kind of bullet-proofing.

### How to use
A great tool to role play, it involves the use of different perspectives or modes of thinking.

**The three roles are:**

*Dreamer*
> *the positive enthusiastic role of the person with the idea*

*Realist*
> *the pragmatist who presents the practical perspective on the plan*

*Critic*
> *the challenger who can be critical of the idea. Hopefully this can be constructive criticism.*

The process can be conducted in several ways. One possibility is for all group members to play all roles in turn. This way everyone gets to understand how the different perspectives can influence the process. Equally valid, and particularly if there are only 4 or 5 in the group, each person can be allocated to one role, with an observer and a scribe appointed to record feedback. Place a role name on each chair and place them strategically in your space.

### How to facilitate
Initially you will need to establish ground rules similar to brainstorming rules and ensure participants stick to them.

An approach to facilitating this technique is to have the 'dreamer' role present the idea/solution, then allow a few moments to reflect (not to discuss), and the 'realist' role responds with the pragmatic perspective. After a few moments again to reflect, the 'critic' offers the critical perspective.

A second and third round are played, and each time the dreamer reinforces or adapts their position considering the other perspectives.

It's important in this technique that all feedback from the critic and realist as well as any amended 'ideas' of the dreamer, are recorded – so it's important to have a scribe.

At the end of the process the scribe and observer give feedback. Again, as in the other divergent techniques in this stage, and in preparing to develop the action plan, include both the solutions and the actions that will enable the implementation to happen.

# Convergent Phase

### Action Planning

The final part of this process is to develop an action plan which will enable implementation to go ahead. Your action plan comes from the selected solution(s) and the outcomes from the bullet-proofing that happened in the divergent phase.

If you used a Cartoon Storyboard during the convergent phase of Idea Generation, add the important targets in each box (Figure 10). Your final version can become your action plan.

### The wrap-up from the CPS process

So, we've taken you through a full process of Creative Problem Solving with some suggested techniques at each phase and advice about facilitation. There's more general advice on facilitation in Section 6.

As a reminder of the process we've taken you through, and to pull it all together, here again is the image of the Creative Problem Solving process (see opposite).

### The key takeaways from this part are:

- Plan and prepare a process that will allow adequate time for divergent and convergent phases. That will allow space for extroverts and introverts to contribute.
- Establish ground rules from the beginning and enforce them.
- Facilitate openly and flexibly. Give the technique time to work.
- Be prepared to ditch a technique if it isn't working.
- Work off site if you can; if not use a different workspace, preferably one without tables to sit around. Chairs in circles, with desks or tables behind for putting any resources on is a better choice.

## STAGE 1  EXPLORE PROBLEM

**OPEN UP**
DIVERGE

**Explore different angles of the problem**
An understanding of the 'issue' is achieved

**CLOSE DOWN**
CONVERGE

**Select key problem to work with**
Frame the problem

## STAGE 2  GENERATE IDEAS AND PLANS

**OPEN
UP**

**Generate ideas to solve the problem**
Many possible solutions/actions have been noted

**CLOSE
DOWN**

**Select preferred options**
Preferred solution(s) selected

## STAGE 3  IMPLEMENT PLAN

**OPEN
UP**

**Review implementation issues and bullet-proof the plans**
Possible barriers to implementation identified

**CLOSE
DOWN**

**Develop action plans**
Agreed actions for implementation

## 5.6 Alternative Process to the CPS

In this section we offer you two alternative approaches that you may find useful. The first is the Six Thinking Hats which is a more logical and rational approach to analysing a problem than those described in Section 5.5. It can also be used in the main stages of the CPS process.

## Six Thinking Hats

### Description
The Six Thinking Hats process helps individuals and teams to organise and classify information about a problem so that its complexity can be better understood. It also enables the team to have a conversation where everyone thinks in the same way – at the same time. As a result, everyone considers the problem from many different points of view. This is very important for a complex problem.

It was developed by Edward De Bono more than twenty years ago, and I, (Tracy speaking here), consider it valuable as it helps everyone to contribute and for a problem or opportunity to be analysed from numerous perspectives. The value of the concept is in separating information, emotions and hopes so that thought processes and discussions can be more easily facilitated.

You can probably remember a meeting which got out of hand because there were different aspects discussed at once and the conversation may have become adversarial. For example, one person may have been discussing the possibilities inherent in the idea while someone else felt the need to be a devil's advocate so kept identifying problems with the idea. The discussions may have become overwhelming, confrontational and/or 'stuck' as a result.

The Six Thinking Hats process supports use of the brain's different modes of thinking. Everybody's information, perspective and feelings are separated into one of six categories for discussion. In each of these directions our brain works to make us conscious of issues being considered, such as our gut instinct, pessimistic judgement or neutral facts. As Edward de Bono himself says,

> *The main difficulty of thinking is confusion. We try to do too much at once. Emotions, information, logic, hope, and creativity all crowd in on us.*

The problem or opportunity is considered in six ways, with each pass associated with a hat of certain colour. Blue Hat thinking is typically considered first. In this phase the current situation/problem or opportunity is described along with the goal for the activity.

The next hat you choose and the type of thinking you engage in depends on the objective of the session – I'll give you a few choices in a moment based on your objectives. But first let's look at the White Hat.

When a team puts on their White Hat they are presenting all the facts, figures and statistics related to the problem. Just the data is discussed here: no opinions allowed. This information should be neutral and objective, and an outcome could be that more objective data is needed.

When we put on our Red Hat the team is encouraged to declare how they feel about the idea or problem. These feelings will include their 'gut instinct', intuition, offering all the emotional stuff 'warts and all'. For example they may say, 'I feel nervous' or 'I feel angry'. (Be careful on time management with this one as sometimes it can be hard to pull in the emotional reactions to the problem or situation.)

Black Hat requires the team to think cautiously as they explore the risks associated with the problem or opportunity. Later, once the risks are identified, a further conversation on the steps to mitigate the risks is important.

Yellow Hat is when everyone thinks about the idea from a positive perspective only. For example, 'What is great about this idea?' This will help to identify the opportunities and possible benefits.

Green Hat requires the team to do their best creative or out-of-the-box thinking. Stretch thinking is applied here to imagine new futures and possibilities. Consider, 'What could be a wonderful outcome here?'

**A summary of the objectives of each 'Hat' phase is provided in Figure 14 below.**

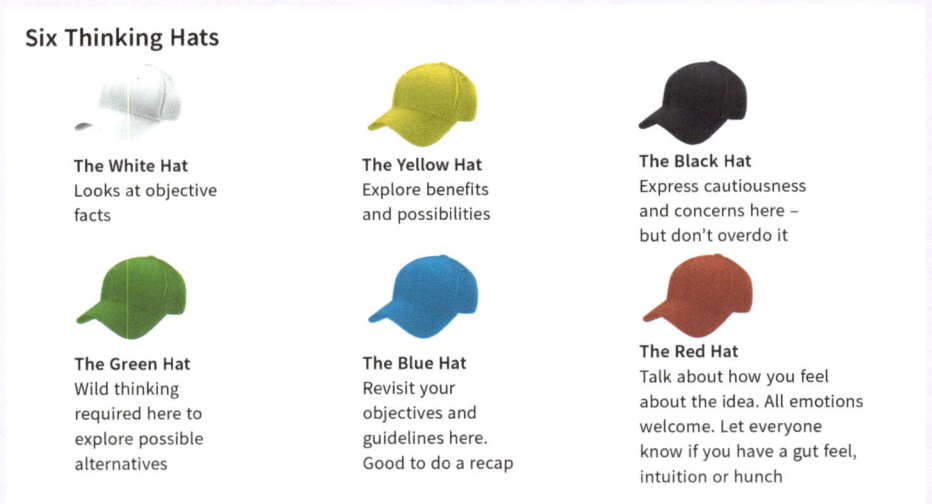

## Six Thinking Hats

**The White Hat**
Looks at objective facts

**The Yellow Hat**
Explore benefits and possibilities

**The Black Hat**
Express cautiousness and concerns here – but don't overdo it

**The Green Hat**
Wild thinking required here to explore possible alternatives

**The Blue Hat**
Revisit your objectives and guidelines here. Good to do a recap

**The Red Hat**
Talk about how you feel about the idea. All emotions welcome. Let everyone know if you have a gut feel, intuition or hunch

**Figure 14** Overview of Six Thinking Hats model by Edward De Bono

### How to use the Six Thinking Hats

As a versatile tool, Six Thinking Hats can be used in a 'normal' meeting as well as in a special-focus event. The process should start with a proposition or problem statement.

As mentioned earlier, the order of discussion for each of the hats will depend upon the team's objective. For example, if the team's opportunity is exploratory or emergent in nature, they might plan just a few hats such as Blue, White and Green – and then the facilitator (or team) can decide which, if other, processes (i.e. Hats) they engage with.

### If you're solving a complex problem, this order works well:

- Solving Problems – Blue, White, Green, Red, Yellow, Black, Green, Blue

- Initial Idea Exploration – Blue, White, Green, Blue

- Strategic Planning – Blue, Yellow, Black, White, Blue, Green, Blue

- Identifying Solutions – Blue, White, Black, Green, Blue

As the Blue hat focuses everyone on the objective of the discussion, we recommend that you start and end with the Blue hat. In turn the team can discuss all the hats together or people can work in pairs and then present their analysis to the team.

After the first Blue hat round, which should take no longer than five minutes, subsequent rounds should last no longer than two minutes. This will keep everyone focused. The discussion points can be captured on a flip chart or similar.

Once the ideas are captured, discuss what surprised people or what new perspectives they gained from the process.

A recommended next step is to vote for the most pertinent points under each hat, perhaps using the Sticky Dot voting method mentioned earlier.

At the end of the exercise the facilitator puts on the Blue Hat to review how well the process worked.

A useful training video for using the Six Hats has been developed by Paul Sloane and can be accessed at

www.destination-innovation.com/tutorial-on-how-to-use-the-six-thinking-hats/

**Resources needed for group work**

- A facilitator. It's best to have someone external to the team so everyone in the team can participate. They will help the team to stay focused on the objective of the discussion.

- Timer and bell.

- It can be useful to have someone as a dedicated scribe if possible. It's best that this is not someone from the team as this would limit their contribution to the discussion.

- Comfortable setting where team can sit around a white board and see each other while the problem is discussed.

- Flip chart paper and sticky dots.

- Visual props such as photos, figures/tables and storyboards.

- Hats. It's great to have hats in each of the six colours – it helps to reinforce the objective of the process.

Below is the wrap on things you should reflect on if you plan to use De Bono's Six Thinking Hats.

| TABLE 7 BENEFITS AND CONSIDERATIONS OF SIX THINKING HATS | |
|---|---|
| Benefits | Considerations |
| Run a practice Six Thinking Hats process with the team on a problem outside their area so that they become familiar with the methodology before they use it for a problem more real for them. | Watch the clock so that discussions are controlled – but be flexible if new and useful areas are explored. |
| Check in on everyone's mindset prior to starting (people arriving in a bad mood will influence the outcomes). | Don't let participants go back to a previous hat, such as the Red hat when you are looking at Green hat ideas. |
| Hold the event off site, to stimulate new thinking in a new space. | |

## Someone Else's Shoes

### Description
Often the best way to obtain new insights into a complex situation is to view it from different stakeholder or customer perspectives. (A stakeholder is someone impacted by the situation). It's similar to the Fresh-Eyes process where you get a perspective from an outsider who may or may not have a stake in the problem being examined.

A simple and powerful technique for thinking differently is metaphorically stepping into someone else's shoes and living their experience. Ask yourself, how well do I know the people impacted by this problem? What are their needs, fears and objectives? What would the best resolution of this problem look like for them? What would be the worst outcome for them?

It's always important to check yourself to ensure that you are considering their perspective and not your own. In this activity you will role play being one of the parties affected by the problem; a great way of building empathy for other stakeholders.

### Before you start
What information do you have about the stakeholder?

**Assess: How objective or subjective is this data?**

If you need to collect more, what's the best way to do this? Through observation, interviews or surveys?

Some organisations video a day in the life of a customer in order to understand how they use their products and services. Others spend time developing detailed personas for each customer segment so that their needs and fears are better understood.

**How to use**

Identify the key customers and stakeholders related to the problem. It could be a customer, partner, a group in your organisation or a competitor.

Plan a role play around a scenario where the problem is discussed. Give all stakeholders an opportunity to share their perspective on the problem.

Discuss what new insights emerged from the process.

Swap roles and do the activity again, giving participants the opportunity to be in several people's shoes.

Identify how to use the new insights to solve the problem.

**Resources needed**
- Information about the customer and stakeholders who have an interest in the problem.
- Place to prepare for and run role plays.

Table 8 below summarises a few things to think about if you use Someone Else's shoes.

| TABLE 8 BENEFITS AND CONSIDERATIONS OF SOMEONE ELSE'S SHOES | |
|---|---|
| Benefits | Considerations |
| If you video the event, make sure everyone is comfortable with this in advance. | Make sure you have a debrief after the role play so that learning is identified. |

Take notes of lessons learned.

## 5.7 Takeaways: Being a more creative problem solver

- Identify whether the problem you are facing is complex (or wicked) before deciding whether CPS is appropriate.

- Plan and prepare a process that will allow adequate time for divergent and convergent phases. That will allow space for both extroverts and introverts to contribute.

- Select both image and word-based techniques to enable both rational and creative processes to work at appropriate points.

- Establish ground rules from the beginning and enforce them.

- Have a structure, but be flexible enough to change during the process. Facilitate openly and flexibly. Give the technique time to work.

- Work off site if you can, but if not then in a different workspace preferably without tables to sit around. Chairs in circles, with desks or tables behind on which you can place resources, works well.

**REFLECTION POINTS**

**Consider participants, objectives and timing when planning.**

**Consider your role in the process: whether you facilitate or use an external facilitator.**

# PART 6
# Being leader, coach and facilitator

In this section we focus on your role as leader, coach and facilitator. Some of these points may have already been discussed, however we want to bring these to your attention now. Be conscious of your behaviour and how it affects others' openness to offering different views and to engaging in different ways of thinking.

## 6.1 Core leadership behaviours that support creativity in your team

Consider this list of behaviours that support thinking differently. Many of these will be familiar to you as they often appear in advice on how to be a great leader.

- Listening actively and carefully to what people are saying – and perhaps not saying

- Reflecting back to a person what you have heard

- Displaying curiosity

- Asking questions

- Inviting team members to participate – particularly when they have been quiet

- Responding positively to new ideas and approaches

- Experimenting or proto-typing

- Showing an openness to taking risks with new ideas

- Spending time analysing a problem in detail

- Capturing and presenting information in a range of ways

- Reflecting on and exploring lessons learned

- Capturing these in a format which can be accessed in the future

- Recognising mistakes as learning points

- Encouraging play

- Providing recognition for effort as well as achievement.

## 6.2 Leader as facilitator

Facilitation is an important and undervalued competence as recognised by one of our interviewees:

### *Facilitation is one of the most underrated skills. Karl*

Here are some general guidelines on facilitating creativity sessions whether you are planning to run a full CPS process or trying out one or two techniques.

We hope that these will help you in planning and facilitating if you intend doing it yourself. If you choose to use an external facilitator, they will help you to be an active participant in the design of the session.

**Timing**
How long do you have and how will you divide up that time?

CPS puts a lot of emphasis on the first stage, Problem Exploration. If you get that 'right' then the other two stages work more smoothly. Therefore, my recommendation would be to allow time roughly in a 40:30:30 proportion to each of the three stages.

Are you going to run the whole process in one day or divide it up into say three sections, running over different days?

The decision will depend upon the time available to you. If you are going off site, which is preferable, then a whole day would be the best way to work.

How experienced are you and the team with creative techniques?

The more experienced you are, the less time you will need to get into the creative mode.

**Place**
Where will you hold the sessions?

As we've already commented, off site is always best as it signals a different way of working. It's hard to change to a creative mode when working in the same environment as your everyday work. If off-site is not an option try to find a space where a conducive atmosphere can be created – perhaps where there are no tables, nor computers, and plenty of wall space to exhibit outputs as you go along.

One of our interviewees, explained that her team went off site when budget allowed, but if there was no budget they had found an area in the basement which had a different feel about it and where they could have a good space for working together creatively.

Wherever you chose to work you will need to review the techniques you plan to use and the resources available at the venue. This should include facilities for posting pictures or other material on walls or boards, and suitable spaces for any messier activities such as collage and painting.

**Choice of technique**
You may have a preference: if you're new to this, stay with something you feel comfortable with until you are able to risk trying something new. A facilitator needs to be able to guide participants and then let them free to work on the technique. If you are nervous about trying a new technique you may be tempted to intervene.

Always choose according to the stage and objective of each session. For example, if you are doing idea generation and divergent techniques, look for techniques that are suitable for this stage.

The individual differences of participants may also be a factor here. Introverts may take longer to think through their inputs. Build in techniques which they will feel more comfortable with, otherwise the extroverts will dominate.

*In groups some people will be louder than others. It is harder in large groups. It's important to let the quieter ones speak. There is a big risk for some when they are in a group. It's important that the quieter people are not overshadowed by the noisier ones. You may have to break group into pairs so that everyone can be a part of the conversation. It's important to give quieter people the opportunity to contribute. James*

A diversity of techniques supports idea diversity. Choose both image and word-based techniques

When introducing the techniques consider how you will warm up and energise the participants.

There needs to be some 'warm up' in order to encourage people to be willing to play. If this isn't attended to, people can be negative. Chloe

You will find examples of ice breakers and energisers below.

In choosing the techniques and planning the sessions, reflect upon whether each technique will work best done individually, in pairs or as a whole group. In the description of the techniques we offer some guidance on these. However, when you choose your options, bear in mind some of the advantages and disadvantages of working in each way.

> ### *Use a combination of individual reflection and group processes to get the best ideas. It helps to eliminate conformity. Charlie*

Working alone will work well if it's an early input around perceptions of a problem, after which sharing in pairs and the whole group will be important.

Working in pairs for some of the exercises can offer a level of support and comfort.

Working as a whole group can produce more ideas, as with brainstorming; however there may be issues around everyone being involved. It will depend upon the group. My advice would be anything beyond six needs to be broken down into smaller groups.

When choosing techniques allow for Fresh-Eye to emerge. As mentioned in Section 3 it's always helpful to have different perspectives and fresh ideas from people who do not have pre-conceived ideas about the problem.

Taking the perspective of Someone Else's Shoes is also helpful. This is where inputs are given from the point of view of another, be it the customer, or a different team, or a different function. Any of the techniques could be used for this. All it requires is that ideas are offered from the perspective of the other. This is very similar to the technique of superheroes in brainstorming.

Here's a final word on creative techniques in general and the aim in facilitating them.

One of our interviewees mentioned the importance of being both focused and relaxed: this is a great aim to bear in mind when introducing techniques. To have a focus for the technique, and to encourage an open, relaxed mind when working through it are also great aims.

### Ice-breakers and Energisers
You'll have noticed that we have mentioned the importance of warm-up exercises a

couple of times. These help to set the tone that this workshop/exercise is different, and that play is allowed. Here, I have divided them into two categories, Ice-breakers and Energisers. You will note that in three of the four I propose that it encourages laughter. Laughter enables energy and playfulness to emerge and is important in creativity.

Be aware however of your surroundings and ensure that any noise doesn't annoy your neighbours!

### Ice-breakers
The purpose of this is to help participants to relax and get to know one another better. Even in an established team this can be helpful.

### The Name Game
Ask participants to stand in a circle and introduce the purpose of the exercise which is to introduce themselves. Begin with yourself, so if I was starting I would say my name, Barbara and use an adjective beginning with B to describe me. So, I might start with Bubbly Barbara. The next person, say Tom, then says something like Trusting Tom, however he also has to say Bubbly Barbara first. Then it goes on - the third person may say I am Super Sarah, after saying Bubbly Barbara, Trusting Tom….

You can probably imagine that this soon descends into laughter and relaxes participants who invariably forget the earlier names!

An alternative ice-breaker could be for each member of the team to share in turn one thing that no-one else knows about them. This is partly a trust building exercise as well.

### Energisers
The purpose of an energiser is to do just that, to inject some energy into the room when people start feeling drained. Of course, getting a coffee may help. However, the playfulness of energisers can inject more than just energy.

### A variation on Musical Chairs
In this exercise there are no chairs taken away however people do get to move around and there is always one chair less than the number of participants.

To start, have one person volunteer, and it can be you as the facilitator. Have all participants sit on a chair in a circle around you. You do not get to sit, you stand in the middle.

You then say all people with – and name a characteristic which is also common to you, like wearing blue jeans at that time - change place. At this, all those wearing blue jeans stand and find a new chair to sit on. Only those not wearing blue jeans can remain where they are. Whilst this is happening you also try and find a chair to sit on.

Whoever is left standing gives the next direction - and the same thing happens again.

It can get very noisy and unruly, so keep it relatively short, maybe 5 or 6 rounds. However, it does lead to a lot of fun and laughter and raised energy.

**Copy My Leader**
This is based on a children's game and again can be fun and encourages playfulness.

Have everyone stand in a circle and you explain that you are going to make a movement, and everyone should copy this until you change the movement. Make it simple to start with, like an arm movement. Then change the movement, add noise, like clapping, and after a couple of changes ask that someone else, anyone, take over but don't specify who that should be. Until this is picked up participants continue with the current movement. This can become very amusing as more people change the movement. Allow for a maximum of 2 to 3 minutes for this exercise especially if it is becoming too noisy and boisterous!

**Briefing participants in advance**
How will you introduce your CPS session?

Setting expectations is important and needs careful thought. You want participants to show up ready to try something new and be prepared to some extent. However, what you don't want are people who have already decided what the 'solutions' are.

**Resources**
- *What resources will you want, or can have?*
- *Lots of coloured pens, post-its and paper for writing and drawing are essential, as are flip chart boards or walls to put paper on.*
- *Ensure that you capture all outputs from the sessions. Taking photos is useful as it captures ideas on flip charts that you can take away and write up. Consider how you will share these later with non-participants.*

## Setting ground rules for the creativity session

This is crucial. You will need to think this through in advance and present them for agreement at the beginning. The purpose of setting ground rules is to enable working and sharing ideas together in a trusting environment where people feel able to take risks and work outside their comfort zones.

**Here are the rules we like to establish:**

- Brainstorming rules: defer judgement, go for quantity, the wilder the ideas, the better, build upon others
- Be constructive – no negativity
- Work with a positive regard to others
- Be flexible and open to others ideas
- Encourage active listening.

You might want to add rules about keeping to time, confidentiality, mobiles off.

Getting everyone's agreement and ensuring a common understanding of the problem is crucial. As is achieving the purpose of setting ground rules which enable working and sharing ideas together in a trusting environment where people feel able to take risks and work outside their comfort zones.

## Key takeaways on facilitation

Have a structure and be flexible enough to change it if necessary. Not all techniques work with everyone and sometimes you need to try something different to achieve the objective of the session. Techniques work best when people become comfortable using them. The mantra of practice, practice, practice definitely applies here.

> *The main barrier is the fact that people are not used to these kinds of techniques and they can be seen as awkward. They need to be used often to progressively prove their efficiency. Julian*

When facilitating a group, start with some warm-up exercises, and also have a couple of short energisers to use later on when energy is starting to flag.

Set out the instructions for the exercise and then stand back and let the participants work with the technique. If you are facilitating, it's important not to step in unless it's about how to do the exercise. Do not try to influence what is happening.

Finally, a word of advice from one of our interviewees:

> *It's also important to let everybody without exception express something, my consideration there is no bad ideas. Simon*

## 6.3 Leader as a creativity coach

Coaching as a leader is a different way of leading a team, quite unlike the normal 'tell' or 'sell' or even 'consult' styles of leadership: Coaching empowers the team members to act in their own right without having to ask for direction all the time.

However, before taking on this role, you need to be aware of some important points.

As a leader you need to ensure that your team are developed sufficiently to be able to manage autonomously or at least know in which areas they can become more autonomous.

In coaching, it's the person being coached who takes on the responsibility for working through, with the help of the coach, what needs to be done and how. The coach does this by asking relevant questions that act as a guide for reflection by the coachee.

For example, instead of stating what needs to be done, a leader as a coach might ask,

> *Tell me about the situation?*
> *Describe what you have done that has worked?*
> *What hasn't worked, what can you do differently?*

*Coaching for being more creative may also need some input from the leader. For example, in order to open up to new ideas, ask*

> *What exercises or tools might you consider using?*
> *and then, 'Have you considered using this one?'*
> *'If so how would you implement it?*

*Earlier in the book, we talked about assumptions. We encourage you, as a leader, to challenge assumptions both in yourself and in team members. Again, consider how to do this in a coaching frame of mind. So, to challenge an assumption, ask permission, 'Is it OK if I offer you a suggestion here?' 'Have you considered the impact of ...?'*

# PART 7
# Pulling it all together

Great. You've made it here. We're hoping you've found value in what you've read about setting the context for individuals and teams, and in the tools and processes to help your team become more creative.

The Creative Problem Solving process is at the heart of the book, describing ways you can take your team through divergent and convergent thinking. It's the bike that will help you to get to your final destination and we hope that you feel comfortable getting in the saddle – although you may feel a little wobbly if you've not ridden before.

As a leader you need to create an environment built on trust. If we had to identify top takeaways from the book, building an environment built on trust would be one of these. It's the bike frame that supports everything else. If you have trust, you will have collaboration and the idea generation process can start.

Use different processes for idea exploration, recognising the different learning and communication styles and preferences of your team. Take a risk and try techniques that push you and your team out of your comfort zone. You'll find that it's worth it!

Access people from diverse backgrounds and with diverse perspectives, which will help support different thinking. Celebrate the diversity, even though it will make the process longer.

Recognise that complex problems require a different type of process and that great ideas take time to incubate.

Finally, if you need further clarification on any of the material or advice on getting started, don't hesitate to reach out to Barbara or myself. Here's how to do this.

**Emails**
**barbara@barbara-wilson.com**
**tracy@tjstanley.com**
**You can find us online at**
**Barbara**
**Twitter @BarbaraAWilson**
**Linkedin** https://www.linkedin.com/in/barbaraawilson/

**Tracy**
**Twitter @tjstanley64**
**Linkedin** https://www.linkedin.com/in/tracystanley1/

Happy Cycling! We wish you the best whatever your final destination.
*p.s. If you've picked up ideas on ways you can help your team to think differently, we'd love you to tell others. One way you can do this is by writing a review.*

# How we wrote this book

We've both worked, coached, facilitated workshops and undertaken research around creativity and thinking differently. Motivated to inspire others to be more creative we decided to capture the best of our experiences in a book. We wanted to help organisations – and by organisations we mean leaders – to build workplaces where people felt safe to explore different approaches to complex problems. We know that as a leader becomes more senior in their organisation, the problems they face are more complex. We've written this book to help this evolution.

We drew on our experience and research to write the book, along with input from leaders who were interested in helping their teams think differently. We applied some of the creative processes mentioned in this book to help us with the thinking, writing and marketing processes.

# Appendix

## Situational Outlook Questionnaire

### Description

Situational Outlook Questionnaire is a useful tool for assessing your team's climate for creativity. Originally developed by Ekvall and enhanced by Isaksen, Lauer and Britz, it provides a way of measuring the climate in your team. The questionnaire assesses nine dimensions by asking questions to provide meaningful information on what is working, what is not, and what needs to be done to make the climate better.

These are the nine dimensions:

**Challenge and Involvement:** Degree to which people are involved in daily operations, long-term goals and visions. Where there is a high degree of challenge and involvement, people feel motivated and committed to making contributions. The climate is dynamic, electric and inspiring. People find joy and meaningfulness in their work. In the opposite situation, people are not engaged, and feelings of alienation and apathy are present. Individuals lack interest in their work and interpersonal interactions are dull and listless.

**Freedom:** Independence in behaviour exerted by the people in the organisation. In a climate with much freedom, people are given the autonomy and resources to define much of their work. They exercise discretion in their day-to-day activities. Individuals are provided the opportunity and take the initiative to acquire and share information about their work. In the opposite climate, people work within strict guidelines and roles. They carry out their work in prescribed ways with little room to redefine their tasks.

**Trust/Openness:** Emotional safety in relationships. When there is a high degree of trust individuals can be genuinely open and frank with one another. People count on each other for professional and personal support. People have a sincere respect for one another and give credit where credit is due. Where trust is missing, people are suspicious of each other, and therefore they closely guard themselves, their plans and their ideas. In these situations, people find it extremely difficult to openly communicate with each other.

**Idea time:** Amount of time people can use (and do use) for elaborating new ideas. In the high idea-time situation, possibilities exist to discuss and test suggestions not included in the task assignment. There are opportunities to take the time to explore and develop new ideas. Flexible timelines permit people to explore new avenues and opportunities. In the reverse case, every minute is booked and specified. The time pressure makes thinking outside the instructions and planned routines impossible.

**Playfulness/Humour:** Spontaneity and ease displayed within the workplace. A professional yet relaxed atmosphere where good-natured jokes and laughter occur often is indicative of this dimension. People can be seen having fun at work. The climate is seen as easy-going and light-hearted. The opposite climate is characterised by gravity and seriousness. The atmosphere is stiff, gloomy and cumbrous. Jokes and laughter are regarded as improper and intolerable.

**Conflict:** Presence of personal and emotional tensions in the organisation. When the level of conflict is high, groups and individuals dislike and may even hate each other. The climate can be characterised by 'interpersonal warfare'. Plots, traps, power and territory struggles are usual elements of organisational life. Personal differences yield gossip and slander. In the opposite case, people behave in a more mature manner, and have psychological insight and control of impulses. People accept and deal effectively with diversity.

**Idea Support:** Ways new ideas are treated. In the supportive climate, ideas and suggestions are received in an attentive and professional way by bosses, peers and subordinates. People listen to each other and encourage initiatives. Possibilities for trying out new ideas are created. The atmosphere is constructive and positive when considering new ideas. When idea support is low, the automatic 'no' is prevailing. Fault-finding and obstacle-raising are the usual styles of responding to ideas.

**Debate:** Occurrence of encounters and disagreements between viewpoints, ideas and differing experiences and knowledge. In the debating organisation, many voices are heard and people are keen on putting forward their ideas for consideration and review. People can often be seen discussing opposing opinions and sharing a diversity of perspectives. Where debate is missing, people follow authoritarian patterns without questioning them.

**Risk-taking:** Tolerance of uncertainty and ambiguity in the workplace. In the high risk-taking case, bold initiatives can be taken even when the outcomes are unknown. People feel as though they can 'take a gamble' on their ideas. People will often 'go out on a limb' to put an idea forward. In a risk-avoiding climate, there is a cautious, hesitant mentality. People try to be on the 'safe side' and often 'sleep on the matter'. They set up committees, and they cover themselves in many ways.

# References and further reading

Amabile, T. M., Schatzel, E. A., Moneta, G. B., & Kramer, S. J. (2004). Leader behaviors and the work environment for creativity: Perceived leader support. *The Leadership Quarterly,* 15(1), 5-32.

Argyris, C. *Ladder of Inference*. 21 July 2014. 21 September 2014.

Claxton, G. (1997). Hare Brain, Tortoise Mind: How intelligence increases when you think less.

Collins, H. (2000). Collins English Dictionary. *Dictionary. com.*

Csikszentmihalyi, M (2008) Flow: *The Psychology of Optimal Experience Harper Perennial Modern Classics*

Dilts, R.B. & Dilts, R.W. & Epstein, T (1994) *Tools for Dreamers; Strategies for Creativity and the Structure of Innovation.* Meta Publications

De Bono, E. (2017). *Six thinking hats. Penguin UK.*

Dul, J., & Ceylan, C. (2011). Work environments for employee creativity. *Ergonomics*, *54*(1), 12-20.

Dweck, C. S. (2007). *Mindset: The new psychology of success*. Random House Incorporated.

Ekvall, G. (1983). *Climate, structure and innovativeness of organizations: A theoretical framework and an experiment.* Farådet, the Swedish Council for Management and Organizational Behaviour.

Henry, J., (2001) *Creativity and Perception in Management*, The Open University Business School

Isaksen, S. G., Lauer, K. J., Ekvall, G., & Britz, A. (2001). Perceptions of the best and worst climates for creativity: Preliminary validation evidence for the situational outlook questionnaire. *Creativity Research Journal*, *13*(2), 171-184.

Jeffers, S. J., (2012). *Feel the fear and do it anyway*. Random House.

Johnson, S., (2010). *Where good ideas come from: The Natural history of innovation.* Riverhead Books

Jong J, P. J., & Den Hartog D. N. (2007). How leaders influence employees' innovative behavior. *European Journal of Innovation Management, 10(1), 41-64*

Mason, R. O., & Mitroff, I. I. (1981). *Challenging strategic planning assumptions: Theory, cases, and techniques*. John Wiley & Sons Inc.

Mencken, H. L. (1949) *The divine afflatus*, A Mencken Chrestomathy Knopf, New York, New York

Meridian Resources Associates. (1997). *Communicating across technology.* San Francisco, CA: Meridian Resources Associates.

Morgan, G. (1994). Imaginization, the art of creative management. *Administration in Social Work*, *18*(4), 132-134.

Morgan, G. (1997). Images of organisation; 2nd. *Auflage, Thousand Oaks, Calif.*

Osborn, A. F. (1953). *Applied Imagination: Principles and Procedures of Creative Problem-Solving*

Parker, M. (1990). *Creating shared vision*. Dialog Intl.

Rittel, H. W., & Webber, M. M. (1973). Dilemmas in a general theory of planning. *Policy sciences*, 4(2), 155-169.

Scott, S. G., & Bruce, R. A. (1994). Determinants of innovative behavior: A path model of individual innovation in the workplace. *Academy of Management Journal*, 37(3): 580-607.

Senge, P. M. (2014). *The Fifth Discipline Fieldbook: Strategies and tools for building a learning organisation*. Crown Business.

Sloane, P. (2007). *The innovative leader: How to inspire your team and drive creativity*. Kogan Page Publishers.

Stanley, T. (2016). *Work environments, creative behaviours, and employee engagement* (Doctoral dissertation, Queensland University of Technology).

Unsworth, K. L., & Clegg, C. W. (2010). Why do employees undertake creative action? *Journal of Occupational and Organizational Psychology*, 83(1): 77-99.

VanGundy, A. B. (1988). *Techniques of Structured Problem Solving*. Springer.

Wendell, O.H. (1899). *The Autocrat of the Breakfast Table*. Houghton

Wiseman, L., McKeown, G., & Covey, S. R. (2010). *Multipliers: How the best leaders make everyone smarter*. New York, NY: Harper Business.

Yukl, G. A. (2013). *Leadership in Organisations*. Pearson Education India.

# Website References

**World Economic Forum**
https://www.weforum.org/agenda/2016/01/the-10-skills-you-need-to-thrive-in-the-fourth-industrial-revolution/

**Ken Robinson Ted Talk – Do Schools Kill Creativity?**
https://www.ted.com/talks/ken_robinson_says_schools_kill_creativity

**New York Times article on remote working**
https://www.nytimes.com/2017/02/15/us/remote-workers-work-from-home.html

**Myers Brigs Type Indicator (MBTI)**
http://www.myersbriggs.org/my-mbti-personality-type/mbti-basics/

**James Brook, The Strengths Partnership Ltd on the Path of Positivity**
http://www.strengthspartnership.com/blog/words-create-worlds-leaders-hr-mind-language/

**Belbins Team roles**
http://www.belbin.com/about/belbin-team-roles/

**Paul Sloane**
www.destination-innovation.com/tutorial-on-how-to-use-the-six-thinking-hats/

# Acknowledgements

While our names are listed as the authors, this writing project benefited from/was powered by the idea input, feedback and support of many people (just like any great creativity project).

**All our thanks**

| | |
|---|---|
| Adel Boucekkine | Jean-Louis Richard |
| Carlo Patteri | Michael Strickland |
| Claire-Marie Chaffin | Kirk Vallis |
| Craig Strong | Sabine Strauss |
| David Stoyle | Serge Niango |
| Gillian Attard | Sheena Stewart |
| Harvey Wade | Wendy Buckley |
| Jean Marc Saint-Pierre | |

Thanks to Emma Wilson for her valuable feedback on an early draft of our book.

# Barbara Wilson by Tracy Stanley

I first heard Barbara speak twenty years ago at a networking event in France. She was polished and powerful and I sensed her passion and values quickly. I soon learnt that she is feisty and never accepts the status quo.

We share a similar background in human resource management and consulting. She has also worked in the corporate world in the engineering, telecoms, clothing and chemical industries before moving into Higher education to teach Organisational Behaviour and Management.

Apart from being my co-author, Barbara is an Executive coach, creativity and leadership facilitator with extensive experience of supporting people and organisations to achieve their potential. She's done a tonne of work with leaders helping them to engage their team and use creative approaches to developing themselves and their business

I learn such a lot from our conversations. We have different styles and we get quite a bit of practice at disagreeing respectfully. Wonderful.

Barbara knows her stuff about human behaviour. She has a BA (hons), an MBA from the Open University, is a Fellow of the Chartered Institute of Personnel and Development and Member of the British Psychological society

She introduced me to the philosopher Goethe. Both Goethe and Barbara inspired me to take steps in the direction of my dreams. I'm so grateful for that.
*Whatever you can do, or dream you can do, begin it. Boldness has genius, power, and magic in it. Begin it now. Goethe*

# Tracy Stanley by Barbara Wilson

I've known Tracy for twenty years. When we met I was impressed by her enthusiasm, optimism and overall strength of character, and we went on to develop the Professional Women's Network based on the Cote D'Azur, which is still flourishing today.

Tracy has a similar corporate background to me, having worked in human resource management and organisational change within travel, technology, government, financial services, mining, education and health sectors. With her expertise across employee engagement, organisational change and intrapreneurship, she is now an entrepreneur where she writes and speaks to inspire others.

Always curious, she has gained qualifications including an MBA and MBus (Research). In 2016, she completed a doctoral thesis at the Queensland University of Technology, investigating how work environments influence creative behaviours and employee engagement.

Having lived and worked in the UK, France, Thailand and Australia, she possesses insights into cultural influences on leadership and employee engagement.

We both share a love of the adventures of The Secret Seven: a small troupe solving mysteries together, often on their bicycles. Their exploits inspired Tracy's career in foreign lands and interest in understanding what makes a great team.

It's been exciting working with Tracy to write this book. Co-authoring a book can be challenging, particularly when the authors have differing views and perspectives. However, the experience has been both motivating and fun!

# Notes

# Notes

# Notes

**Notes**

# Notes

# Notes

www.ingramcontent.com/pod-product-compliance
Lightning Source LLC
Chambersburg PA
CBHW041305210326
41598CB00005B/31